D0064548

"Eric Bargerhuff demonstrates that many well-known verses are commonly misunderstood and, consequently, misused. He explains how attending to historical, cultural, and literary context, word meaning, genre, and translation options can help us avoid interpretation and application errors and gain a deeper appreciation of the Bible's purpose and message."

—Richard Schultz, Blanchard Professor of Old Testament, Wheaton College, and author of *Out of Context: How to Avoid Misinterpreting the Bible*

"The scholarship behind looking at the verses is impeccable. . . . This is a book that should be a part of any vital study library."

—*Portland Book Review*

THE MOST MISUSED VERSES IN THE BIBLE

Surprising Ways God's Word Is Misunderstood

ERIC J. BARGERHUFF

BETHANY HOUSE PUBLISHERS
a division of Baker Publishing Group
Minneapolis, Minnesota

Published by Bethany House Publishers
11400 Hampshire Avenue South
Bloomington, Minnesota 55438
www.bethanyhouse.com

Bethany House Publishers is a division of
Baker Publishing Group, Grand Rapids, Michigan

Printed in the United States of America

Library of Congress Cataloging-in-Publication Data
Bargerhuff, Eric J. (Eric James)
    The most misused verses in the Bible : surprising ways God's Word is misun-
derstood / Eric J. Bargerhuff.
        p. cm.
    Summary: "A pastor and Bible scholar discusses well-known Bible verses
that are commonly misused or misunderstood and presents their proper interpretation and application"—Provided by publisher.
    Includes bibliographical references.
    ISBN 978-0-7642-0936-9 (pbk. : alk. paper) 1. Bible—Criticism, interpreta-
tion, etc. 2. Christian life—Biblical teaching. I. Title.
BS680.C47B37 2012
220.6—dc23   2011038418

Cover design by Dan Pitts

In keeping with biblical principles of creation stewardship, Baker Publishing Group advocates the responsible use of our natural resources. As a member of the Green Press Initiative, our company uses recycled paper when possible. The text paper of this book is composed in part of post-consumer waste.

To all those who stay at their desk for hours, week after week, studying so that when they stand behind the pulpit to bring the message to God's people they can "get it right." God's Word will not return void.

Books by Eric J. Bargerhuff

The Most Misused Verses in the Bible
The Most Misused Stories in the Bible

Contents

1. Where It All Began   13

2. Judging Others   25

   "Do not judge, or you too will be judged."—Matthew 7:1 (NIV 1984)

3. Plans to Prosper You and Not to Harm You   33

   "'For I know the plans I have for you,' declares the Lord, 'plans to prosper you and not to harm you, plans to give you hope and a future. Then you will call upon me and come and pray to me, and I will listen to you. You will seek me and find me when you seek me with all your heart.'"—Jeremiah 29:11–13 (NIV 1984)

4. Where Two or Three Are Gathered   43

   "For where two or three are gathered together in my name, there am I in the midst of them."—Matthew 18:20 (KJV)

5. Ask for Anything in My Name   55

   "Whatever you ask in my name, this I will do, that the Father may be glorified in the Son. If you ask me anything in my name, I will do it."—John 14:13–14

6. Working All Things Together for Good   63

*"And we know that for those who love God all things work
together for good, for those who are called according to his
purpose."—Romans 8:28*

7. If My People Who Are Called by My Name   71

*"If my people who are called by my name humble themselves,
and pray and seek my face and turn from their wicked ways, then
I will hear from heaven and will forgive their sin and heal their
land."—2 Chronicles 7:14*

8. Jesus As the Firstborn Over All Creation   79

*"He is the image of the invisible God, the firstborn of all
creation."—Colossians 1:15*

9. Money Is the Root of All Evil   87

*"For the love of money is a root of all kinds of evils."—1 Timothy
6:10*

10. No More Than You Can Handle   93

*"God is faithful, and he will not let you be tempted beyond your
ability."—1 Corinthians 10:13*

11. Train Up a Child   101

*"Train up a child in the way he should go; even when he is old he
will not depart from it."—Proverbs 22:6*

12. I Can Do All Things   109

*"I can do all things through Christ who strengthens me."
—Philippians 4:13 (NKJV)*

13. An Eye for an Eye   117

*"If there is serious injury, you are to take life for life, eye for eye,
tooth for tooth, hand for hand, foot for foot, burn for burn, wound
for wound, bruise for bruise."—Exodus 21:23–25 (NIV 1984)*

14. The Prayer Offered in Faith   123

*"The prayer offered in faith will make the sick person well."
—James 5:15 (NIV 1984)*

Contents

15. Repent and Be Baptized   133

> *"Repent and be baptized every one of you in the name of Jesus Christ for the forgiveness of your sins, and you will receive the gift of the Holy Spirit."—Acts 2:38*

16. Guarding Your Heart   139

> *"Above all else, guard your heart, for it is the wellspring of life."*
> *—Proverbs 4:23 (NIV 1984)*

17. Where There Is No Vision   145

> *"Where there is no vision, the people perish."—Proverbs 29:18*
> *(KJV)*

18. Lifting Up the Name of Jesus   155

> *"And I, when I am lifted up from the earth, will draw all people to myself."—John 12:32*

19. Conclusion: Handle With Care—Using Scripture Appropriately   161

Notes   169

Acknowledgments

I GREW UP ON A STEADY DIET of topical "feel good" sermons, until one day when I entered college, someone handed me a cassette tape of John MacArthur Jr. preaching the Word of God in expository fashion. I remember saying to myself, "What is *that*? . . . I *want* that, and not only do I *want* that, I want to *do* that." My then eighty-five-year-old college Bible professor, Dr. J. Ray Klingensmith, once said that "people are starving for the Word of God and they don't even know it, but when they hear it, believe it, and get a taste of it, it feeds their soul like nothing else can."

This I believe to be true. And this is why I love the ministry. There is no greater privilege than to proclaim, teach, and unpack the Word of God before God's people and all others who have ears to hear. But one thing my doctoral mentor and teacher, Dr. Wayne Grudem, said, was this: "You better get it right, because people will believe you, and as teachers we will all have to give an account one day." He was spot-on, and it inspired me to strive for faithfulness in "rightly dividing the Word of truth."

This essentially is what this book is all about—learning to properly interpret and apply the truths of the Bible in a faithful, God-glorifying way so that we don't distort the Word and will of God. So many throughout my life have served as exceptional examples of how to handle Scripture, and there is not enough room to acknowledge them all.

But in a small way, I wish to acknowledge those who have aided me in this project. There are portions of this book that landed in a sermon series at Clearwater Community Church, where I served as senior pastor for over six years. The feedback, response, and support that I received from the body of Christ there encouraged me beyond measure, and I am thankful for the privilege of serving the Lord with them.

I am deeply indebted to my initial proofreader, Karen Ancrile, who gave much time and effort to reading and critiquing the initial drafts of this manuscript. Her feedback and suggestions were remarkable, and I can't thank her enough for her service.

I further wish to thank my editor Jeff Braun for his excellent leadership, direction, and skill in working with this manuscript. It is a privilege to partner with the fantastic people at Bethany House Publishers, whose flexibility and professionalism are second to none.

All thanks and glory go to our Lord Jesus Christ, whose words will never pass away. I look forward to the skies parting soon.

CHAPTER 1

Where It All Began

A N EYE FOR AN EYE . . ."

"Where two or three are gathered together in my name, there am I in the midst of them . . ."

"Do not judge, or you too will be judged . . ."

These common phrases—derived from the bestselling book of all time, the Bible—have often been misunderstood and misused. But when interpreted and applied properly, these and other God-inspired truths have shaped cultures and countless generations of people throughout history.

Indeed, the Bible is a *life-changing book*. It tells us who God is and how he is working in our world today. It reveals how he has been faithfully at work in the past and what his will is for the future. But perhaps the most important thing about the Bible is that it is a work of God that possesses great power, written so that we might believe and experience the salvation and eternal life that comes through faith in Jesus Christ.

According to its own testimony, the Bible is inspired (or "breathed out") by the Spirit of God, and is "profitable for teaching, for reproof, for correction, and for training in righteousness" (2 Timothy 3:16). Therefore, the Bible has authority over us. But this authority is not merely derived by how it functions or by what place it holds in our lives, but rather from its claim to be the very voice and revelation of God.

Believers regard the Bible as the place where God continues to speak truth into our lives, a "living and active" Word—the sufficient foundation for all of the life and practice of the believing Christian.

Written by nearly forty human authors over a period of 1,500 years, the Bible is remarkably consistent and lacks contradiction. Throughout the years, attempts have been made to usurp its truthfulness and integrity, but it has stood the test. Even archaeology has empirically verified its historicity and accuracy. And when all the facts are known, the Bible will continue to show itself to be without error and the foundation of all truth.

However, if mishandled and used inappropriately, the Bible can turn into a *dangerous book*.

Adolf Hitler, for example, was widely known to take the words of Jesus out of context and use them for propaganda purposes. In 1922, in a speech in Munich, Germany, Hitler hijacked the words of Jesus for his own agenda as he sought to eradicate the Jews. Hitler referenced times when Jesus rebuked the corrupt spiritual leadership of his day, such as when he cleared the temple by force after chief priests and others in charge made it into a marketplace for thieves, thereby corrupting Passover.

The horror of reading how Hitler twisted Jesus' words and actions is immeasurable. The following is an excerpt from his speech:

> My feelings as a Christian point me to my Lord and Savior as a fighter. It points me to the man who once in loneliness, surrounded only by a few followers, recognized these Jews for what they were and summoned men to fight against them. . . . In boundless love as a Christian and as a man I read through the passage which tells us how the Lord at last rose in His might and seized the scourge to drive out of the Temple the brood of vipers and of adders. How terrific was His fight for the world against the Jewish poison![1]

Hitler took words that Jesus had directed toward a select group of wicked men in his day, and with one broad stroke, painted an entire people group with the same brush, hanging the label POISON on all of them.

I realize this is an extreme example, but it shows how much damage can be done when the Bible is taken out of context and abused. Yet even on a much smaller scale, well-intentioned Christians have misquoted the Bible and misunderstood its meaning, leaving behind a trail of confusion and faulty decisions pertaining to God's will for one's life. Many a theological heresy has resulted from the misuse or misinterpretation of Scripture, and this can happen no matter how noble the intentions of its interpreters.

This all leads to the purpose of this book: to come face-to-face with some of the most misused verses in the Bible, verses that have often lost their context today and taken on new meanings outside the stories and teachings of Scripture. Indeed, phrases like "an eye for an eye," or "where two or three are gathered," as well as "do not judge, or you too will be judged," are a few of the more commonly misunderstood and misused verses. The task will be to bring these verses of Scripture and others back into their proper context so that they can be interpreted and applied correctly.[2]

To be sure, times change and applications may vary, but the *original author's meaning and intent and the subsequent principles derived from that are fixed and eternal*. It is therefore necessary that we understand what these excerpts actually meant when they were written so we can apply them properly today. It is only then that we may say we are faithfully using God's Word as the Holy Spirit intended.

Nothing New Under the Sun

Have you ever been misquoted? Has something you've said been taken out of context and used against you? It can be more than frustrating. When it happens, there is a burning desire to set the record straight, to justify and defend ourselves against false information that may paint us in a negative light.

These situations can start quite innocently. Imagine a loved one overhearing a conversation you are having with someone on the phone. Because they are only hearing one side of it, they don't have the context of what is being said, or why. Assumptions can be made and inappropriate conclusions drawn.

In today's information age, the world is swarming with photo-shopped pictures and edited sound bites, bits of information that can easily be misinterpreted and misused if taken out of their original context. We see this in political circles, where candidates may find their words being edited or used in a way to undermine their integrity, or to make them look foolish or extreme in their views.

All of this reeks of injustice and puts the age-old question of "what is true?" in the forefront of our minds. But like the writer of Ecclesiastes has so aptly said, "There is nothing new under the sun" (1:9). One could argue that misquotes, false information, and misinterpretations have been around since the appearance of the serpent in the garden of Eden. It was there that Satan sought to undermine God's Word. And the strategy and tactics he used are still perpetuated, at many different levels, by people today.

Genesis 3

Our first parents, Adam and Eve, knew nothing but innocence and blessing as those who were made in God's image. God created a virtual paradise for them, a garden teeming with plant life and animals, a harmonious existence that God had masterfully woven from a work of creation that he himself declared "very good" (Genesis 1:31). It was here that Adam and Eve were charged with the command to rule over God's creation, to subdue the earth, and to multiply in number. They enjoyed perfect fellowship with God and each other while they lived in obedience to God. But, as we know, that would all change.

God gave specific commands to Adam concerning the trees in the garden. The fruits of the trees were healthy and good, with the exception of one: He was not to eat from the tree of the knowledge of good and evil, lest he die. What he did with these commands was a test of Adam's obedience and character, and it was his obligation to teach them to the woman God would give him; at the time the commands were issued, Eve did not exist.

Satan, a fallen angelic being, arrived on the scene in the form of a crafty serpent. He had several goals in mind: to destroy what God had made by perverting the truth so as to gain control over and enslave those who were made in God's image. He wanted to be their master, to control their destiny. He wanted to have the place that only God himself rightly deserves, and in order to accomplish this, he had a scheme bent on undermining God's voice, the source of truth and life. The account begins:

> Now the serpent was more crafty than any other beast of the field that the Lord God had made. He said to the woman, "Did God actually say, 'You shall not eat of any tree in the garden'?" (Genesis 3:1).

Notice Satan's initial tactic. His first blow was to cast suspicion and doubt on the Word of God: *"Did God actually say . . . ?"* Then the crafty serpent took things a step further. He intentionally misquoted God: "Did God actually say, 'You shall not eat of *any tree* in the garden'?" The serpent took God's original command, that they were not to eat of a particular tree in the garden, and expanded it to sound like a prohibition against eating from *any tree* in the garden. So the very first question in the entire Bible is nothing less than a misquotation of God's Word.

But to Eve's credit, she recited back to him the proper command, even though she bought into some of the confusion by adding to it a bit:

> And the woman said to the serpent, "We may eat of the fruit of the trees in the garden, but God said, 'You shall not

eat of the fruit of the tree that is in the midst of the garden, neither shall you touch it, lest you die'" (Genesis 3:2–3).

Eve corrected the serpent by stating that they could eat from *all* the trees of the garden except for the one in the middle (presumably the "tree of the knowledge of good and evil"). Yet Eve added that they were not even allowed to touch it, though God did not say that in his original command.[3]

But that was not the ultimate source of Eve's undoing (or Adam's). A stronger, more lethal attack was about to be launched as Satan sarcastically questioned the legitimacy and goodness behind moral restrictions and boundaries on human behavior:

> But the serpent said to the woman, "You will not surely die. For God knows that when you eat of it your eyes will be opened, and you will be like God, knowing good and evil" (Genesis 3:4–5).

It's as if Satan were asking, What's with the rules? Why have boundaries? Weren't you made to be free? Can't you see that God is afraid you will end up being equal with him? The seeds of doubt that would lead to death were sown in front of her. The trap was set.

But note what he tried to do. The serpent wanted her to see God's restrictive commands in a new light, to perhaps understand them differently from what was originally intended, and *to give them a new context.* Theologians often suggest that the desire to be equal with God is the very temptation to which Satan himself was guilty of succumbing.

The serpent's tactic was nothing less than a direct assault on the Word of God, when he suggested, "You will not surely die! Your eyes will be opened! You will be like God!" (an outright lie from the "father of lies," John 8:44). The serpent attempted to portray God as a selfishly insecure, risk-taking deity who is irrationally afraid that his creation will no longer need him unless restrictions are placed upon them. He further baited her with the idea that unrestricted freedom and human reason are the highest of all virtues. And if that were not enough, he appealed to the prideful idea that one could be like God, or even be his own god.

Ironically, many world religions, cults, and forms of false teaching throughout history, and today, perpetrate some of these same ideas: Knowledge is the highest of virtues, one can become their own god, and unrestricted human freedom is a must. Satan's strategies and tactics have changed little throughout history. And they can all be traced back to the book of Genesis.

Of course we know the results of all of this. Eve took the fruit and ate it, as did Adam, who was with her at the time (3:6). Their "eyes were opened," they realized they were naked (covered only with shame), and they rushed off to make themselves coverings. Now their natural bent was to go inward, to withdraw and hide from God, the One who had created them and designed them for intimate fellowship. They were meant to reflect his glory, but instead sought a glory of their own.

At the heart of all human sinfulness is lawlessness and the prideful appeal to be our own god. To determine our own destiny. To have our own way. To throw off restrictions and doubt the integrity of God's goodness. To doubt the trustworthiness of his Word. And all we need to do in order to start down that path is to give Scripture a new context, twist its meaning, or interpret it in a way that appeals to the supremacy and glory of man.

The serpent successfully taught Adam and Eve the dance of disobedience, and it delivered them over to death.

The Pattern Continues

If anyone was ever aware of Satan's prolific efforts to misuse the authority of Scripture, it was Jesus Christ. In the New Testament, we see Satan using the same strategies as before. He attempts to exploit Jesus in a moment of human weakness with a full frontal assault upon the Word of God.

The context is simple. In Luke 4, Jesus is at the beginning of his ministry. He is baptized by John the Baptist and led by the Spirit of God into the Judean wilderness to be tempted and tested by the devil. All of this is in preparation for Jesus' earthly ministry. It is here that Satan goes after him, tempting him first with food and then with a temporal power over the earth (arrows aimed at both body and soul). Satan is once again seeking to be equal with God by bringing God down to his level.

However, the sinless Christ refutes the first two attacks by appealing to Scripture written long ago by God's servant Moses and recorded in the book of Deuteronomy. He knows that the tool for victory in moments of temptation is God's Word, and he wields the "sword" with precision to fight off his attacker. Then the devil tries a third and perhaps his most creative assault. He uses the very weapon Jesus is using, the Word of God, and tries to manipulate a section from Psalm 91 for his own purposes:

And [the devil] took him to Jerusalem and set him on the pinnacle of the temple and said to him, "If you are the Son of God, throw yourself down from here, for it is written, 'He will command his angels concerning you to guard you, and on their hands they will bear you up, lest you strike your foot against a stone'" (Luke 4:9–11).

What's interesting here is that Satan not only knows and uses the Word of God, but this time (unlike in the garden), he chooses to quote it correctly. In other words, it is not a misquote or an incorrect citation of the verse, but it is a *misuse* of it.

Instead of seeing this beautiful section of Psalm 91 as it really is—a *general promise by God* to care for his people—the devil inappropriately applies it to a situation that seeks to test God's sovereignty. He's enticing Jesus to engage in reckless behavior, and then claiming that if indeed God's Word was true, God should protect him. But this is an abuse of the Word of God.

It would be like someone tempting you by saying, "Hey, if God is sovereign, what's the big deal if you drive a hundred miles an hour up and down the highway? He'll take care of you, right? Nothing should ever happen, unless it's your time." But that line of thinking and argumentation is foolish. It abuses the idea of God's sovereignty by putting God to the test. And Jesus sees right through it and once again thwarts the attack by quoting Scripture (Deuteronomy 6:16) and applying it accurately:

And Jesus answered him, "It is said, 'You shall not put the Lord your God to the test'" (Luke 4:12).

It would seem that the apostle Paul was right. In Ephesians 6, he instructed the church to put on the armor of God so that they may stand against the devil's wicked schemes. Comparing this to the armor of the Roman soldier (whom he may have been looking at while he was writing), he told the church to put on the belt of truth and the breastplate of righteousness. They were to embrace the message of the gospel, which was like wearing shoes that would give them good footing in the battle. They were also to pick up the shield of faith and put on the helmet of salvation.

For the most part, all these are defensive weapons. But one piece of the armor is meant for offense. Paul called it the Sword of the Spirit, or the Word of God, capable of demolishing strongholds, those satanically inspired lines of thinking and argumentation that are inherently hostile toward the truths of God—i.e., false teaching.

When used rightly, the Bible is the source of the Christian's power and might within the battle. And believe me, we are now more than ever in a spiritual battle for the truth in this dark world.

So as we begin this journey through some of the most misused verses in Scripture, we must first realize that misquoting and misusing God's Word has been one of Satan's key strategies and tactics in his attempts to undermine the rightful reign and authority of God in the world. In fact, this is how Satan led humanity down the path of destruction.

When human beings fall into this temptation today by their own misuse or manipulation of Scripture, we only perpetuate the lies that can lead others astray. Therefore, it is all the more important that we investigate and rightly "divide the word of truth" in its proper context with as much precision and accuracy as possible.

CHAPTER 2

Judging Others

"Do not judge, or you too will be judged."
—Matthew 7:1 niv 1984

I**T IS A PHRASE** that has been used countless times during
contentious conversations or in defensive moments when
someone is confronted about their behavior: "Do not judge,
or you too will be judged." These famous words from Jesus
are recited by many but profoundly misunderstood. One
could easily argue that Matthew 7:1 is by far the most fre-
quently misapplied verse in the entire Bible, used and abused
by both Christians and non-Christians alike.

Those who mishandle this verse often use it as a "shield
for sin,"[1] a barrier to keep others at bay, allowing them to
justify living as they please without any regard for moral
boundaries or accountability. Their objections sound like
this: "Aren't we all sinners? What gives us the right to make
moral judgments about someone else? Isn't that God's job?"

However, when we take a closer look at the context of Matthew 7 and the teachings of the rest of Scripture, it is clear that this verse cannot be used to substantiate unrestrained moral freedom, autonomy, and independence. This was not Jesus' intent. He was not advocating a hands-off approach to moral accountability, refusing to allow anyone to make moral judgments in any sense.

Quite the opposite, Jesus was explicitly rebuking the hypocrisy of the Pharisees, who were quick to see the sins of others but were blind and *unwilling to hold themselves accountable* to the same standard they were imposing on everyone else. We'll unpack this further in a moment.

But first, let's zero in on Matthew 7:1. It is found in Jesus' Sermon on the Mount, the place in the Bible where Jesus teaches what it means to live faithfully as a committed follower of Christ, one who pursues holiness out of reverence for God. Jesus is proclaiming a high moral standard that is consistent with what it means to live as a citizen of the kingdom of God.

In other words, those who repent and place their faith and trust in Jesus alone for their salvation become "children of God," are adopted into God's family, and become members of the spiritual kingdom he has established on earth. Believers who live in this kingdom are called to live differently, and Jesus is explaining what that looks like in a very practical sense. His words are not hard to understand as he sets up a strong moral ethic that reflects what it means to love God with all your heart and your neighbor as yourself. It is here that Jesus addresses the issue of hypocrisy. For he says:

> Do not judge, or you too will be judged. For in the same way you judge others, you will be judged, and with the measure you use, it will be measured to you.

26

Why do you look at the speck of sawdust in your brother's eye and pay no attention to the plank in your own eye? How can you say to your brother, "Let me take the speck out of your eye," when all the time there is a plank in your own eye? You hypocrite, first take the plank out of your own eye, and then you will see clearly to remove the speck from your brother's eye. (Matthew 7:1–5 NIV 1984)

I can't but wonder if Jesus was looking right at the Pharisees when he said this. Many times throughout the Gospels, Jesus rebukes the Pharisees for their blatant hypocrisy and impossible man-made standards. They were notorious for condemning the shortcomings of others when all the while they were the ones who stood condemned because they were doing the very same things.

How ridiculous. Jesus said that judgment always reciprocates. In other words, the measuring stick they used to measure the lives of others will be the same measuring stick held up against their lives by God himself. Consider this: It is one thing to be judged by your fellowman, but quite another to be judged by God himself. The hypocritical Pharisees were in danger of the latter.

Notice that Jesus says the hypocrite will be the one with the bigger problem. Why? Because their sin was not merely comparable to a speck of dust; it was more like a wooden plank (quite a difference). And they refused to take it out.

What this means is that the greater judgment is reserved for the one who has purposefully overlooked his own mammoth sin while pointing out the smaller sins of others. Jesus emphatically says this must change, so he gives two commands: *Stop judging others in a hypocritical fashion, and get the sin out of your own life.*

Yet let's be clear. Jesus is not suggesting that we have no right to make moral judgments about human behavior, and he is certainly not suggesting we have no right to hold others accountable. He doesn't condemn mutual accountability and moral responsibility and the need to address sin in the church—he addresses hypocrisy.

But it makes little sense to approach a Christian brother or sister about their specific sin (even if you should rightly do so) if you are committing the very same sin and are unwilling to address it or break free from it.

For example, you hear another believer cursing and in humility you gently and lovingly correct him in private, but not a moment later you get on the phone with a friend and share some juicy gossip about someone in church. Do you correct someone else's tongue, but are not willing to correct and restrain your own?

Or imagine a father concerned about how his teenage daughter dresses when she goes to the mall (he wants her to have a sense of propriety, and he understands the struggle males can have in this area). Does he have the right to be concerned? Yes, of course. As a responsible father and mature adult, he has every right to draw up moral boundaries for his children that are in keeping with the principles of Scripture (in this case modesty).

Right after his daughter leaves for the mall, imagine this same father alone in the house. He immediately turns on his computer and begins surfing the Internet for pornography. One minute he is addressing his daughter's need for appropriate modesty (and rightly so) and the next minute he is reveling in immodesty and sexual fantasy with his own eyes and heart. This, my friends, is hypocrisy, and Jesus condemns this sort of behavior. A father should not set up a standard for his daughter that he is unwilling to follow.

Unfortunately, much damage has been brought to the reputation of the church by Christians who say one thing and do another. This is not to say we can ever be perfect, but it is of utmost importance that we live lives of consistency and integrity in order to safeguard the name of Christ, whom we represent, as well as the reputation of his church.

The truth of the matter is we should all be grieved about sin in our lives. And when we see it, we should address it, confessing it and forsaking it out of reverence for God. It is only when we are consistently doing this ourselves that we are qualified and able to address the sins in the lives of our brothers and sisters in the church, which we must do as well.

The Bible makes it clear that it is our duty to spur one another on to live lives that please God. First, our lives should give evidence that we have truly repented of our sin and received Christ by faith. Then from time to time, as necessary, we are also called to mutually correct, rebuke, and encourage one another in love.

Again, no one will reach perfection in this life, but *together* we are to wage war against and forsake the sin that results from living in our fallen flesh. We are to "take off the old life," so to speak, and "put on the new," growing in holiness out of reverence for God. But the reality is we can't accomplish this without the help of the indwelling Holy Spirit and the mutual encouragement and accountability of our fellow brothers and sisters in Christ. We can't do this alone; we need each other!

This then, is why the apostles called us to help one another in our struggle with sin. For example, James says:

My brothers, if one of you should wander from the truth and someone should bring him back, remember this: Whoever turns a sinner from the error of his way will save him from death and cover over a multitude of sins. (5:19–20 NIV 1984)

Paul said something similar in the book of Galatians:

Brothers, if someone is caught in a sin, you who are spiritual should restore him gently. But watch yourself, or you also may be tempted. Carry each other's burdens, and in this way you will fulfill the law of Christ. (6:1–2 NIV 1984)

Notice that both James and Paul assume two things. First, there will be times when fellow believers will wander off the straight and narrow path. Second, they assume that other Christians, out of love, will seek to come alongside that brother or sister in an effort to bring him or her back from the error of their ways and save them from the destructive power of sin (see Jesus' method for doing this in Matthew 18:15–17).

Since we have been commissioned to proclaim a message of repentance and faith to those *outside* the church who need to hear the good news, certainly we need to proclaim the same message of repentance and faith to those *inside* the church.

Therefore, Jesus does not forbid all moral judgment or accountability. Rather, he forbids harsh, prideful, and hypocritical judgment that condemns others outright without first evaluating one's own spiritual condition and commitment to forsake sin.

It is my contention that the popular misuse of "do not judge" reveals just how far the discipline of sound biblical study has slipped in recent years. More than that, it sheds light on the state of our culture, a culture that seeks to avoid accountability and responsibility for personal actions.

This current trend and mentality runs counter to the teachings of Scripture. For the collective teaching of the Bible insists that those who are created in the image of God are morally responsible to God and to one another. So to use "do not judge" as a means of dismissing oneself from moral responsibility would be to interpret it in a way that pits it against the rest of Scripture.

We should remember that "all Scripture is God-breathed," or inspired by the Holy Spirit, and as such it is without error and never contradicts itself (because God never contradicts himself). Therefore, it is always wise to interpret a given passage of Scripture by comparing it with the principles and teachings found elsewhere in Scripture. This provides a healthy check and balance and helps us avoid misinterpretations, logical inconsistencies, and inappropriate applications.

CHAPTER 3

Plans to Prosper You and Not to Harm You

"'For I know the plans I have for you,' declares the Lord, 'plans to prosper you and not to harm you, plans to give you hope and a future. Then you will call upon me and come and pray to me, and I will listen to you. You will seek me and find me when you seek me with all your heart.'"

—JEREMIAH 29:11–13 NIV 1984

CHURCH CAMP. Of all my summer activities growing up in rural Indiana, camp was my favorite. One week each summer I would attend a small evangelical church camp along a lake in a beautiful stretch of farmland widely known for its Amish population, in Shipshewana, Indiana. It would be the place where I would experience some of the most profound moments of spiritual growth in my young adult life.

And each year, when camp came to an end, it was sad to say good-bye to my newly formed friendships, but memories would live on through the black-and-white group picture of all campers, counselors, and cooks that was taken early in the week and handed out on the last day.

This was where I was introduced to a new Christian concept—the "life verse." Let me explain.

On the back of the group picture, most friends would write a few kind words and then sign their name. However, a select few listed a Bible verse. John 3:16, Philippians 4:13, and others were popular—any verse that had special meaning to my friends, verses they intended to "build their life upon."

On the way home in the car, I was eager to look up the verses that my friends had written next to their names. It felt like a treasure hunt, a journey of discovery to see which verses were their personal favorites. Seeing how exciting all this was, I decided it was necessary to find my own "life verse." And the one I chose is just as popular today as it was back then—Jeremiah 29:11–13.

What a great verse to pull out of the Bible and use as my own! It was easy to memorize. Not too difficult to understand. A powerful message. A great promise. What's not to like about it? Prosperity. Protection. Hope for a great future. These are all things that any Christian would want to see become a reality in his or her life. It seemed to echo the American Dream, with God's endorsement behind it.

It quickly and conveniently became not only my life verse, but my subconscious expectation for how I thought God intended to bless my life *right here and now,* just as long as I did what he wanted, as long as I committed myself to seek after him "with all my heart."

But the question is: Is this an appropriate use of this verse, to put God on the hook for a life of prosperity and blessing that fits my timeline and my definition? The answer lies in a closer look at the context of Jeremiah 29.

This time in biblical history was a season of despair. Life was anything but rosy for God's people, the Israelites. Their kings and spiritual leaders were filled with corruption. The people themselves had disobeyed God's commands and had intermarried with some of the surrounding pagan tribes who had led them astray to worship other so-called gods. They had compromised their character and broken the covenant that God had made with them through Moses.

God had had enough. Though there were a faithful few among them, the people as a whole had turned their backs on him. And as was often the case when this sort of thing happened, God would raise up a prophet from among them who would serve as his spokesman.

Enter Jeremiah the prophet, God's chosen messenger.

Now, the role of the prophet often varied. They were often charged with preaching and teaching, advising kings and leaders, and predicting the future. But this time, God's prophet had a daunting task—to proclaim judgment and wrath upon the people of God. They were to be conquered by their enemies and carried off into exile for a very long time, and Jeremiah was charged with delivering this message.

However, this was not the only message God's people would hear. There were also competing and contradictory messages from false prophets, prophets who for selfish purposes were eager to tell people what they wanted to hear. In Jeremiah 28, a false prophet named Hananiah emerges, and he is preaching a much softer and different message than Jeremiah, a message that was sure to be instantly popular.

As the predicted judgment and exile begins, Hananiah falsely prophecies that this judgment of God is relatively minor and is due to last for only *two years*, a direct contradiction to Jeremiah's previous proclamation that the judgment and exile will last for *seventy years* (see Jeremiah 25:11).

So who is right? Jeremiah is. He confronts Hananiah face-to-face and eventually tells him that God will judge him for his false claims and that he will soon die as a result of his lies. Jeremiah says:

> Listen, Hananiah! The Lord has not sent you, yet you have persuaded this nation to trust in lies. Therefore, this is what the Lord says: "I am about to remove you from the face of the earth. This very year you are going to die, because you have preached rebellion against the Lord" (Jeremiah 28:15–16 NIV 1984).

And without delay, the story concludes with a short but definitive statement:

> In the seventh month of that same year, Hananiah the prophet died. (v. 17)

Jeremiah's prophecy concerning Hananiah prevails, and Hananiah's "prosperity gospel" (telling people what they wanted to hear) falls by the wayside. It is false.

All this leads us back to Jeremiah's original prophecy—that God's people will go into exile for seventy years. It is a devastating word. To be sure, the majority of people won't survive long and the rest will have to endure slavery in a foreign land, displaced from their homes, for the remainder of their lives. Even the "faithful ones" among God's people will go into exile.

Jeremiah is so moved by the thought of this terrible reality that he decides to write a letter to those who will at least survive the initial trip into exile. He has a word from the Lord, who wants to prepare them and their descendants for the next seventy years in Babylon (modern-day Iraq). Though it will never be their true home and they will be forced into slavery, the Lord nevertheless encourages them to settle in, build houses, plant gardens, marry, and have children—to make the best of a bad situation.

They are instructed to pray for their captors, knowing that if their captors prosper, they will inevitably prosper as well. But they were to avoid being deceived once again by the false prophets still bent on telling lies to people. These deceivers excelled in flattery, made false promises, and preached messages that were all about pursuing self-centered dreams at the expense of following God, twisting the truth.[1] They were not sent from God.

Truth be told, God's people were looking at seventy years of hard labor, a season of fatherly discipline that would last well beyond their lifetimes, all the while being dominated and subjected to the humiliation of being slaves to their enemies. It would be a hard life.

However, Jeremiah does give the people some good news. And here is where my personal "life verse" shows up:

> This is what the Lord says: "When seventy years are completed for Babylon, I will come to you and fulfill my gracious promise to bring you back to this place. For I know the plans I have for you," declares the Lord, "plans to prosper you and not to harm you, plans to give you hope

and a future. Then you will call upon me and come and pray to me, and I will listen to you.

"You will seek me and find me when you seek me with all your heart. I will be found by you," declares the Lord, "and will bring you back from captivity. I will gather you from all the nations and places where I have banished you," declares the Lord, "and will bring you back to the place from which I carried you into exile" (Jeremiah 29:10–14 NIV 1984).

With this context, there are a few things we should notice right away. First, God is speaking to the Israelite nation of Judah here. This is his plan for the nation, not necessarily a personal promise that is directed to any one person per se. It is a "corporate" promise. Therefore, we should be cautious about grabbing it out of its context and inappropriately applying it to individual believers in the twenty-first century. God is talking about his plans to once again restore his people, prosper them, and literally bring them back from Babylonian captivity!

Second, this is a promise for God's people who *will exist seventy years from now*. The majority of people who hear this promise from Jeremiah's lips will never see it fulfilled in their lifetime. They will likely perish in exile before it comes to fruition.

Therefore, the current exiles should shed off any expectation of looking for a short-term I-deserve-the-best-right-now kind of blessing from this. They were due to endure seventy years of pain and heartache from this captivity.

All this means the prophecy of prosperity and hope was directed toward a future people—those who would be born in exile and emerge from that place much later, the children and grandchildren of the present-day exiles.

So was it a legitimate move for me to take Jeremiah 29:11–13 and use it as my life verse? I think the answer to that is clearly no. Let me explain.

Remember, in my mind I thought this verse would work great for my personal dreams of having a smooth, prosperous, and materially blessed life just so long as I sought after God "with all my heart." I felt that at the very least God was obligated to make my immediate future into a thing of beauty.

I envisioned a great job after college, a comfortable lifestyle, good health—a future *defined on my terms*. I had no problems manipulating the biblical text to suit my own preconceived notions of "blessing" while at the same time giving God my timetable for these things to be realized.

But in doing this, I was violating the context and completely missing the fact that God was talking to a nation (not an individual), a nation that had to go through seventy years of heartache and exile before there was any hope of freedom from captivity. And if it could not be used as a promise for the immediate future of those who first heard it, then it should not be used for my immediate future either.

So then, is there anything from this prophecy that I could still apply to my life today? Yes. Though it is true that the promise of a "future hope" did not guarantee blessing in the short-term sense, it nevertheless still has practical application for them and for me in the ultimate, eternal sense.

The richest and greatest fulfillment of this prophecy is to be realized in a *spiritual way*. This promise ought to bring a great sense of joy to the believer who longs for the "future hope" of experiencing eternal life with God, a restoration that will be experienced in the fullest sense. It is there where we will experience prosperity and protection in abundance, as we are "gathered back" to him.

My immediate "American Dream" could not be substantiated by these verses. When I was young, I wasn't thinking of an overall spiritual application in the eternal sense. I wasn't thinking of spiritual prosperity, spiritual protection, or the spiritual hope of an eternity in heaven with God. I was thinking in primarily materialistic terms, in the here and now.

Once I realized my error, I was somewhat disillusioned and disappointed. It caused me to reflect and to put myself in the shoes of the people who initially heard these words on their way into exile. What if it was God's will for me to have a terrible life by human estimations and standards (like they were going to have) only to be rewarded abundantly with a glorious eternal life later after I'm dead? Could I handle that? And would I still love, serve, and seek after God with the same intensity?

Even Jeremiah, the prophet who delivered these words, had a life that was less than stellar according to our mindset. He was hated, forced from his home, thrown into prison, and tossed into a mud pit. So even for him, this magnificent prophet, the hope for a prosperous and glorious future was more to be realized in the hope of heaven itself than it was to be experienced in the temporal life of the here and now. Reading Hebrews 11, you can see that many of God's people in history had to have the same kind of future hope. Many of them suffered horribly in this life, and yet they lived by faith with the hope of a fuller salvation in a future they could not yet see.

As a believing New Testament Christian then, I can still use Jeremiah 29, but I must apply it appropriately. Without a doubt, a future "heavenly hope" exists for those who have placed their faith and trust in Christ alone for their salvation. This, to me, is the best application of these verses for one who lives by faith today.

But this doesn't mean that everything about it is reserved for our future in heaven. I would also argue that a whole host of blessing and prosperity can come to us in the here and now. But these are primarily *spiritual blessings*—blessings like reconciliation, forgiveness, peace with God, fellowship in the church, and love. Blessings like the fruit of the Spirit, answers to prayer, and joy in worship.

But if we make the mistake of redefining the phrase "plans to prosper you and not to harm you, plans to give you hope and a future" with our own preconceived notion of what that ought to look like for our lives today in the material sense, then we've overlooked and hijacked the context to suit our own human needs and desires.

Now, this does not negate the fact that God might choose to bless us with a great paying job, a beautiful family, and a healthy life on account of his grace. But the bottom line is we should never expect those things to happen or seek to appeal to the promise of Jeremiah 29:11–13 in order to substantiate our expectations. We have no right to hold God hostage to a promise that we have misunderstood.

Friends, in the end, we should never be looking and living for our own glory in this life. Instead, we should be living for God's glory now and waiting for the glory that we will receive from him in the life to come. The Bible says we should consider ourselves as aliens and strangers in this world. God will fulfill his promises, yes, but not all of his promises were meant to be fulfilled the way we want them to be fulfilled in this life, and we cannot twist Scripture around in order to make that happen, or to make Scripture work for us the way we want it to. We have to live by faith. And those who do will receive what he promised. And when we seek him with all of our heart, we will certainly find him.

I've grown up a lot since church camp, and I still believe that it's permissible for someone to choose for themselves a life verse. But let's agree to study it in context first, lest we make the catastrophic mistake of misusing and misapplying it. Jeremiah 29:11–13 contains some great promises, but if I use it to demand the American Dream from God, then perhaps I should also be willing to literally endure seventy years of captivity first (if that's what God should choose).

I think it's better to use it to inspire us to look for the spiritual life that is truly life now, while trusting in the future hope of the life that is yet to come.

CHAPTER 4

Where Two or Three Are Gathered

"For where two or three are gathered together in my name, there am I in the midst of them."

—MATTHEW 18:20 KJV

HAVE YOU EVER experienced a time when something took place and at that very moment you knew it would become a lifetime memory?

Many people remember where they were when President Kennedy was shot in 1963, or when the space shuttle *Challenger* exploded in 1986, or where they were during the terrorist attacks on September 11, 2001. On the more positive side, memories like your first kiss, high school graduation, your wedding day, or the birth of your first child are all significant moments that are quickly and easily burned into our minds.

But sometimes lifetime memories are made of simple things—nothing traumatic or dramatic. For me, one of those everyday events occurred several years ago when my then four-year-old son Joshua and I were running errands together. We started to have one of those simple but profound conversations that surface from time to time.

It was a beautiful sunny day, and there were white puffy clouds scattered everywhere in the blue sky. As we were driving along, Joshua started in with the questions, like four-year-olds often do:

"Dad, where is God?"

"Well, he's everywhere, Joshua," I said.

"Then why can't I see him?"

"Well, God's here on earth and God is also in heaven, but you can't really see him until you get to heaven. But he's still here with us now. In fact, he's all around us."

"Is God up in the trees?"

"Yes, if you go up in a tree, God is there."

"Is he in the sky?"

"Yes, he's in the sky."

"Is he in the clouds?"

"Yes, Joshua, God is in the clouds." (I sure could tell his little mind was going.)

"Daddy?"

"Yes, Joshua."

"I want to see God come out of the clouds."

That last statement hit me and I felt myself tearing up as I told him, "So do I, Joshua, so do I . . . one day we will." A simple inquisitive conversation had turned into a moment of worship for me, all from the mind of a young boy who desired to understand.

So it begins at an early age with simple questions: Where is God? Is God with us? Why can't I see him? Of course, we adult Christians know that God is spirit and that God is invisible. We know that the Bible teaches us that he is omnipresent. In other words, God (in his entire being) is present everywhere within his creation (yet is fully distinct from it). He is not limited by space and time. This is the implication of what David said in Psalm 139:7–10, when he wrote:

Where can I go from your Spirit? Where can I flee from your presence? If I go up to the heavens, you are there; if I make my bed in the depths, you are there. If I rise on the wings of the dawn, if I settle on the far side of the sea, even there your hand will guide me, your right hand will hold me fast. (NIV 1984)

David believed that God was everywhere at all times. He couldn't escape his presence.

But this is not the only way the Bible speaks of God's presence. Perhaps the most dramatic way God reveals his presence is in the person of Jesus Christ. This is the miracle known as the incarnation, the moment when God entered into human history and took on human flesh so as to redeem those who believe in his life, death, and resurrection from the dead.

In a much different way, we also know the Spirit of God (fully God himself) has chosen to reside in the hearts of those who trust in Christ for their salvation. Those who believe in Christ receive the gift of the indwelling Holy Spirit and experience God in a very real and personal way. He not only lives with us but he also lives *within* us.

So it's fair to say that God does indeed manifest his presence in ways that are truly knowable and discernable. And most often when we read of God's presence in the Bible, it is accompanied with the idea that wherever he is, there is blessing.

All of this brings us to a verse that is often recited in Christian circles—one that is widely taken out of context and misused. How many times have you been to a prayer meeting or a worship service and heard Jesus' words from Matthew 18:20?

> For where two or three are gathered together in my name, there am I in the midst of them. (KJV)

It is a great promise, to be sure. Christ communicates to us that when the church has gathered, they can rest assured he is spiritually present with them. But the question is this: In the context of Matthew 18, for what purpose is the church gathering? Is it for prayer? For worship? For fellowship? It might surprise you to realize that it is for none of the above.

Now, let's be fair here. Certainly when Christians gather for prayer, worship, fellowship, or even evangelism, they can take courage and have confidence in the promise of Christ that he would always be with them, even "to the very end of the age" (Matthew 28:20). So in general, we have every reason to believe that he is with us in an individual sense *and* in a corporate sense.

But the passage in Matthew 18 has a specific nuance to it. It is not talking about prayer meetings. It is not talking about worship. In fact, it is not talking about generic Christian fellowship either. Jesus is talking about church discipline.

In Matthew 18, Jesus is instructing the disciples on how they and all who will follow him should handle situations of interpersonal sin and conflict. His instructions about this immediately follow his parable about the lost sheep (which emphasizes restoring someone who has gone astray) and precedes the parable of the unmerciful servant (which is about being willing to cancel and forgive an outstanding debt).

Therefore, the themes that are present in this context are forgiveness, restoration, and reconciliation with a brother or sister who has sinned against you or who has gone astray. Jesus lists several practical steps that should be taken to reconcile or restore a broken relationship, a relationship breached or shattered because of sin. The first step is a private one:

> If your brother sins against you, go and show him his fault, just between the two of you. If he listens to you, you have won your brother over. (Matthew 18:15 NIV 1984)

Essentially, Jesus is teaching that interpersonal sin and conflict should not be ignored or dismissed, because Christians in general should be committed to maintaining healthy, wholesome, and fully reconciled relationships. After all, this is ultimately why Christ died, so that we first could be reconciled with God and second, reconciled to one another. So we must guard and protect our relationships from sin, especially those relationships between believers.

Some Bible translations omit the words *against you* so the text simply reads, "If your brother sins, go and show him his fault." This is because some ancient manuscripts don't carry the words *against you* in the text. But either way, whether the sin is committed "against you" or not, it is still necessary for Christians to address the issue of sin in the church. For even as Paul says in Galatians 6:1:

> Brothers, if someone is caught in a sin, you who are spiritual should restore him gently. (NIV 1984)

Therefore, Jesus prescribes an initial step of a personal and private conversation between Christians, the goal of which is forgiveness and reconciliation. It is a necessary confrontation and conversation that should be done in humility and love. Keeping the issue private and in the smallest possible community is ideal so that any misunderstandings may be cleared up, or for reconciliation to take place in a way that doesn't allow the sin to spread to others.

Furthermore, if it is cleared up, forgiven, and settled at this level, it is unlikely to become an issue that is gossiped about or discussed in unhealthy ways among others. Ideally, this is how all interpersonal sins and conflicts should be handled so that the case can be closed in step one.

However, this is not always possible. Jesus stated that if things can't be resolved at this level, it is necessary to include others. In Matthew 18:16 he says:

> But if he will not listen, take one or two others along, so that "every matter may be established by the testimony of two or three witnesses" (NIV 1984).

There are many purposes for this. First, it adds a level of seriousness to the need for reconciliation. Second, witnesses can ensure the confrontation is handled appropriately if the matter should necessarily proceed to the next level (and this should happen only if step two fails). Third, these two or three additional believers can serve as objective third parties who could come alongside and assist in the process of forgiveness and reconciliation.

Jesus is obviously teaching that unrepentant sin is a serious matter among Christians. And the apostle Paul would later warn the church in Corinth to handle sin matters quickly and expediently, lest "a little yeast [work] through the whole batch of dough" (1 Corinthians 5:6 NIV 1984). In other words, sin that goes unchecked or ignored can be devastating to the witness of the church and can be destructive to relationships within the Christian community. In fact, it may unnecessarily influence others to sin as well!

As similarly stated before, if the incident can be resolved here at this level (step two), then those who are involved should rejoice, agree to keep it private, and promise not to bring it up again. But in more severe cases, where forgiveness, reconciliation, and restoration don't happen, the matter must necessarily proceed to a more somber step three:

> If he refuses to listen to them, tell it to the church; and if he refuses to listen even to the church, treat him as you would a pagan or a tax collector. (Matthew 18:17 NIV 1984)

Here then is the widest circle of accountability possible. What was initially private has now become a more public issue. And here is where the spiritual maturity of the church will be put to the test. Logically, it would seem that the church leadership would be made aware of the situation first so attempts at reconciliation could be made at that level. Perhaps some of them were already involved at step two. But either way, if reconciliation is still not attained, Jesus essentially commands that the problem be brought before the membership.

Why? Because unrepentant sin is a serious matter for the one who is refusing to acknowledge and turn from it. Furthermore, it is at this level that the broadest possible efforts can be made to attempt to reach out to someone who has gone astray. Here is where everyone who has a relationship with the unrepentant can reach out to them in an attempt to "win them back." This is where the church truly embraces what it means to be a forgiven and forgiving community.

Admittedly, not many churches today are willing to practice this step, mainly because they misunderstand its motive or confuse it with some form of inappropriate judging or punishment. But none of that is true. Just like we stated in a previous chapter, the church has an obligation to make moral judgments on cases of unrepentant sin within the church (1 Corinthians 5:12). Moreover, none of this should be seen as punishment, since Christ already received the full punishment for our sins on the cross.

Therefore, we have no choice but to see this as an act of grace, a desperate attempt to reach out and restore a fallen brother or sister who has wandered astray. Remember, this follows Jesus' parable about the lost sheep, and so this is what Jesus is saying the church should be committed to—loving the lost sheep that has gone astray by going out to look for it. The goal here is reconciliation, not punishment. Mercy not only comes to God's people but it proceeds *through* God's people as instruments of his love.

Imagine the rejoicing that would fill the church if indeed this step ended up being successful, if the unrepentant came to repentance and was fully restored to God and to his church. Like the prodigal son returning to his father, there would be rejoicing, celebration, and thanksgiving (Luke 15:11–22). I would suspect that such an event would transform a congregation. Jesus knew this, and I suspect this is why he prescribed it as a command.

But that which is ideal doesn't always become a reality. And Jesus knew this too, and so he told the disciples that if the unrepentant refuses to listen or respond to the loving attempts of reconciliation that proceed from the church, then the church would have no choice but to recognize that this person has chosen to harden their heart and exclude themselves from the church due to their refusal to turn and receive forgiveness. And in Jesus' day, this would be equivalent to seeing them as a pagan or a tax collector (tax collectors were often corrupt in the Roman system of the time). These would have been people who were clearly outside the recognized community of faith.

The church would have no choice but to formally remove them from the fellowship. This doesn't mean that everyone who remains in the church is perfect. We're all sinners. But that's not the issue. The issue is about the one who hardens his or her heart toward their sin and refuses to acknowledge and turn from it. When that happens, the church is obligated by none other than Christ himself to dismiss them from the recognized community of faith. This is a somber and humble but necessary step.

As Christians, our goal should be never to give up on someone. So even if the church has to move to exclude someone from the fellowship, they should still be attempting to reach out to that person and win them to the Lord.

Here then is where our oft misunderstood verse finds its proper context. After establishing the church's authority and heavenly sanction to take such action, Jesus promises his presence in a unique way. Here then is the passage in its entirety:

> Again, I tell you that if two of you on earth agree about anything you ask for, it will be done for you by my Father in heaven. For where two or three come together in my name, there am I with them. (Matthew 18:19–20)

Jesus is saying that whenever the church is pursuing and is involved in a reconciliation process with someone who has refused to repent, they can rest assured that God's blessing is with them in their efforts. In other words, as the church renders judicial decisions on matters of right and wrong that are based on the truth of God's Word, they should be confident that they are doing the right thing and that Christ himself is right there with them, spiritually present in their midst.

After all, he is the God of reconciliation. And he is the one who has commanded them to be agents of reconciliation as well. The church is acting on God's behalf, and therefore has divine sanction as it seeks unity and asks for God's blessing in something that is surely difficult. This then is the true meaning and context for the phrase "where two or three are gathered." It is all about God's presence in judicial matters of reconciliation.

Today, when I hear Matthew 18:20 misused, I don't immediately run to correct the person who said it. They usually mean well. For it is true that when two or three believers *are* gathered, or even when one thousand or twenty thousand believers are gathered, our omnipresent God is there with them.

But the same can be said for someone who is seeking God's face in private. Indeed, Jesus himself taught in his Sermon on the Mount that we should be regularly practicing prayer in the confines of our "prayer closets." For the heavenly Father, who sees what is done in secret, will reward us (Matthew 6:6). God is surely with us.

The bottom line is this: Matthew 18:15–20 is really a challenging passage to apply. Dealing with matters of sin can be tough. But for those who seek to be faithful to God in addressing it, they can count on God's unique presence to bless their efforts.

We should all be eager to gather as believers in the presence of the Lord to worship him, pray to him, fellowship with him, and experience his grace. And to that end, let us be diligent. Indeed we are his people, and as Matthew 18 teaches, we are his agents of forgiveness and reconciliation as well.

CHAPTER 5

Ask for Anything in My Name

"Whatever you ask in my name, this I will do, that the Father may be glorified in the Son. If you ask me anything in my name, I will do it."

—JOHN 14:13–14

IT WAS A SACRED MOMENT, and I didn't want to make a mistake. I knew the day would come, and finally, as the youngest of three children, it was now my turn to say the dinnertime prayer.

Like many children who grew up in a Christian home, I first learned to pray from watching and listening to my parents and older siblings. Traditionally, whenever my family sat down for the evening meal, my father was the one who would pray since he was the head of the family. I always got a kick out of how he would pray in simple language at home, and then when called upon to pray in church, he would turn on some kind of "King James Version" with lots of "thees" and "thous." Maybe it was the pressure of praying in public, but either way I was impressed and knew he was sincere.

I was about five years old the day my father gave me the opportunity to pray at the table. I jumped right in and prayed the best prayer I could muster. But when it was over, all I heard was laughing. Soon it became clear what the hubbub was about. I didn't realize it at the time, but I had closed my prayer with the same words my father would use whenever he would finish praying. After thanking God for the day and the food, I had confidently "landed the plane" with the words "and God bless my wonderful wife, daughter, and sons. In Jesus' name I pray. Amen." When everyone started laughing, I didn't know if I should be horrified or join in. And when I realized what I had said, my face turned beet red. I had definitely made a memory.

Where did *you* learn how to pray? Can you remember? Was it from a grandparent, parent, or friend? Perhaps you have never been taught. If so, you're not alone. Everyone must begin somewhere, and this was true for Jesus' disciples as well. Luke writes:

> Jesus was praying in a certain place. When he finished, one of his disciples said to him, "Lord, teach us to pray, as John taught his disciples" (Luke 11:1).

We're not told which disciple asked for guidance, but it doesn't really matter. They all needed to learn, and it is evident that even the followers of John the Baptist were eager to learn from John as well.

But as Jesus taught his disciples about prayer throughout the course of his ministry, he taught them something specific that has often been misunderstood in Christian circles. Jesus told the disciples that when they ask for things, they should ask the Father *"in my name."*

But what does that mean? Does it mean that asking in Jesus' name gives the prayer an extra boost of sorts, somehow increasing the chances of that prayer being heard and answered? Is it like a magical formula that guarantees we will receive whatever we ask, no matter what, as long as it is prayed "in his name"? These are some common misconceptions.

I remember mistakenly thinking in my youth that if these three words were not attached to the end of *every* prayer, then the prayer would be illegitimate, or that somehow God could not hear it. It was a rather naïve understanding to say the least.

So what did Jesus mean when he advocated that we pray in his name? First, as we look through the Scriptures, we discover that this phrase is used in a variety of contexts.

For example, Jesus talked about welcoming disciples (who are like little children) "in my name" (Matthew 18:5). He spoke of assembling together for judicial action "in my name" (Matthew 18:20). And he spoke of miracles done, cups of water given, and the Holy Spirit being sent "in my name" (Mark 9:39, 41; John 14:26). Apparently Jesus had much more in mind than prayer when he spoke about the power of his name.

To be sure, to do any of these aforementioned things "in his name" means that we do them in a manner that is consistent with who Christ is, what he taught, and all that he stands for (his kingdom purposes). It is to do them in accordance with

God's will, and ultimately for his glory. This is very important for us to remember as we approach the text where Jesus spoke about asking for anything "in my name."

It is best to go to the place where Jesus uttered these words, cite it in its context, and allow other Scriptures to aid in our interpretation. The words of Christ are found in John 14:13–14, but let's begin with verse 12:

> Truly, truly, I say to you, whoever believes in me will also do the works that I do; and greater works than these will he do, because I am going to the Father. Whatever you ask in my name, this I will do, that the Father may be glorified in the Son. If you ask me anything in my name, I will do it. (John 14:12–14)

Jesus is speaking to his disciples at the Last Supper in what is a rather long evening of drama, dialogue, teaching, and prayer. It is here that Jesus makes these astonishing statements. First, he tells them that whoever believes in him will do the works that he does, and more than that, they will do even "greater works."

On the surface, this may be difficult to understand, but Jesus is surely not saying that the disciples will have more supernatural power than he had.[1] He is God, and to interpret it that way does not make sense. The key to interpreting "greater works" is linking it with the final phrase, "because I am going to the Father."

Jesus is about to tell the disciples that upon his return to the Father (which will happen after his death and resurrection), they will receive the gift of the Holy Spirit, which will have major implications for them and their future ministry. Not only will the Holy Spirit supernaturally empower their ministry, but because Jesus has returned to the Father, they will have the distinct advantage of hindsight and be able to point back to the finished work of Jesus Christ, who will have died and risen again by that time.

This picture of Christ and the purpose of his coming will be fuller than what early believers understood during Christ's earthly ministry, when it was somewhat veiled.[2] This clarity, along with the Spirit's power, will result in many more converts than were seen during Jesus' earthly ministry, and in this sense the good news of the gospel will be made more widespread.

Here then is what "greater works" means. The number of "physical" miracles that were performed by Jesus will pale in comparison to the number of "spiritual" miracles that will take place when both Jews and Gentiles are converted to Christ in this Spirit-filled church age.

And it is here within this new era of ministry that Jesus promises his help:

> Whatever you ask in my name, this I will do, that the Father may be glorified in the Son. If you ask me anything in my name, I will do it. (John 14:13–14)

In other words, their powerful ministry is bound to be aided by answered prayer. And the key to the effectiveness of their prayers is that they will be asking "in his name," which again is to pray in a manner that is consistent with who Christ is, what he taught, and all that he stands for (his kingdom purposes).

In essence, it is to pray in accordance with God's will—ultimately for God's glory—"that the Father may be glorified in the Son." Then as the disciples pray "in Jesus' name," with those motives in mind, they can rest assured that their prayers will be answered and that Jesus himself (*"I* will do it") will be assisting them from heaven in their ministry efforts.

When people learn to pray like this, with these motives and with this perspective, it is amazing to see how God answers their prayers. Prayers turn from a selfish focus to a more God-centered, God-glorifying focus, and the results are dramatic. In fact, this is the clear promise of 1 John 5:14–15:

> And this is the confidence that we have toward him, that if we ask anything *according to his will* he hears us. And if we know that he hears us in whatever we ask, *we know that we have the requests that we have asked of him.*

Our first inclination usually is to pray in a way that fits with what we think is best, or according to the results we desire. For example, if we are in pain, or receive an unfavorable diagnosis, we will usually immediately pray for God to take away the pain or completely heal whatever is ailing us. We pray for our circumstances to change.

It is not wrong to pray for these things, but it would be better to pray something like this:

> Lord, I know you have a purpose for everything you bring into my life, and my prayer is that you would be glorified in whatever way seems best. Please teach me what you want me to learn from this so that my faith will grow. Please help me to see what your sovereign purposes might be, so that I may rejoice in your plan and rely upon your grace. But Lord, if it would be pleasing to you, I do ask that you would bring relief from this pain and healing from this hurt, for this is my desire. Either way, I trust you and I pray that your will be done. I ask this in Jesus' name. Amen.

This, I believe, is a healthy way to pray. It may not be perfect (I am growing in my understanding of how to pray), but it does display trust, teachableness, and reliance upon God. It also seeks to humbly accept his sovereign plan, whatever that may be. At the same time, there is no hesitation to ask God for the desire of your heart, knowing that if God's answer is no, or not yet, God will give sufficient grace to meet the challenge.

Our goal in prayer is to see God glorified no matter what. Our goal is to see things his way, so that our will aligns with his. And once this happens, our prayers are filled with power. They will be answered, and with confidence we can say, "We know that we have the requests that we have asked of him" (1 John 5:15). This, my friend, is what it means to ask "in his name."

So it is safe to say that praying "in his name" is not a mere mechanical phrase we can invoke simply to make sure that any and all requests we make are heard by God. Neither does it have anything to do with giving our prayers an extra boost to heaven so that they find additional favor with God. And it is not a wild card that can be played so that we forward a personal agenda and "force God's hand" on anything that is not part of his plan.

I smile when I think about my father and his steadfast prayers for his "wonderful wife, daughter, and sons." I was never blessed with a daughter, but God did give me the gift of a beautiful wife and two sons. And my prayer is that as I pray for them, I will learn what it truly means to pray in Jesus' name.

CHAPTER 6

Working All Things Together for Good

"And we know that for those who love God all things work together for good, for those who are called according to his purpose."

—ROMANS 8:28

HAVE NEVER ONCE doubted that God was good. Even as a small boy when I read C. S. Lewis's *The Chronicles of Narnia,* I knew Aslan the Lion (who was a figure of Christ) wasn't a safe lion, but he was *good.*

This somehow seems easier for many people to accept when they are younger. But as we grow older and the challenges and scars of life become reality, some find it harder to see the biblical perspective found in the old saying "God is good all the time, and all the time, God is good."

To say that God is good is to say that within the heart of God, he is morally excellent and kind. His heart is true, his love is pure, and his kindness is seen in the goodness and mercy that he gives in abundance. For as David said at the end of Psalm 23:

> Surely goodness and mercy shall follow me all the days of my life, and I shall dwell in the house of the Lord forever. (Psalm 23:6)

But this idea of God being good and being full of goodness is often put to the test during difficult times, and it brings to mind a verse that is often misconstrued and misunderstood even to the point where some have questioned the "good" nature of God himself. The verse is Romans 8:28, and it was written by the apostle Paul in what is perhaps one of the most glorious and familiar sections in all of Scripture:

> And we know that for those who love God all things work together for good, for those who are called according to his purpose. (Romans 8:28)

So there it is: "All things work together for good." But what does this promise really mean? Does it mean that whatever happens in life, everything is going to be fine?

When the doctor calls and the cancer has returned, is it true that all things work together for good? When the police officers show up at your door on your son's prom night, is it true that all things work together for good? When you lose your job, your marriage of thirty years begins falling apart, or your stock portfolio takes a dive right before you retire, is it true that all things work together for good?

Where do you find the good when the doctor says, "I'm sorry, there's nothing more we can do but make her comfortable"? For many people, Romans 8:28 merely seems like an unkept promise, or worse, a flat-out lie.

But coming to that conclusion—a false conclusion—stems from a misinterpretation of what Paul is actually saying. As always, it is important to take a closer look at this verse in context so that we can understand and apply it appropriately.

First, we should know that the apostle Paul is talking here to *believers,* those who have trusted in Christ for their salvation and have been given the gift of the indwelling Holy Spirit. This will become even more evident when we dissect the verse.

Thematically, in this section of Scripture, Paul has just set forth the idea that believers in Christ are set to receive an inheritance from God and are bound for glory, which puts our sufferings in perspective. In fact, Paul says the sufferings we experience in life pale in comparison to the future glory that awaits us as people of faith.

And we long for that time to arrive when Christ returns and both body and soul are delivered from the fallen flesh and eventually glorified.[1] The Bible says we along with creation inwardly "groan" for it.

Yet until that day comes, we have to rely upon the Holy Spirit in all of our day-to-day weaknesses. During times when we don't know how to pray about a situation, we have to rely on the Holy Spirit to help and intercede for us. But even though we don't always know how to interpret our day-to-day struggles or even know how to pray about things due to our human limitations and weaknesses, there is something that we do know:

We know that for those who love God all things work together for good, for those who are called according to his purpose. (Romans 8:28)

See the contrast there? There is much we don't know, but there is one big thing we do know—*all things work together for good*. So the first question is: For whom? Do all things work together for good for everyone? No. It is very specific. Paul says this is a promise for Christians only. It is for those who love God, or saying it another way from God's angle, those who are called (to salvation) according to his purpose.

This should tell you right away that not everyone is able to claim this promise, because not everyone believes in Christ. So Christians should be careful in using this verse as a promise for a friend or a loved one who is not a believer. Please be aware of that.

The second question is: What does it mean to say that all things work together for good? Is Paul defining the word *good* the way we might be tempted to define it today? Is *good* short for general success? Health, financial security, or personal happiness? If so, I have news for Paul: God does not always seem to be working all things together for good for Christians in that way. As you well know, life can be full of tragedy, even for Christians. Loved ones die. People get cancer. Jobs are lost. Children get hurt. (Otherwise, everyone would want to be a Christian.)

So what then is the ultimate good that Paul is talking about? Well, the answer lies in the very next verse:

For those whom he foreknew he also predestined to be conformed to the image of his Son. (Romans 8:29)

There you have it. That's the ultimate good for which God is weaving and working all things together. The good of *making us more like Christ*, or as Paul said it, being "conformed to the image of his Son." This means that we as Christians have to junk our superficial fleshly definition of what's good as defined in modern-day terms and trade it in for a theologically robust definition of good.[2] In other words, in this instance, our definition of good should be God's definition: "to be conformed to the image of his Son"—being made more like Jesus.[3]

In this sense, "all things" that happen in the Christian life are designed for this purpose—the ultimate good of bringing glory to God, of advancing his kingdom purposes, and making us more holy, filling us with love, bringing about humility, developing our patience, cultivating our trust in God . . . the list could go on. God is using these circumstances (remember, "all things") to grow us spiritually and make us more like him until the day he calls us home to heaven or he returns to earth, whichever comes first (the day we are "glorified"—see verse 30).

Essentially then, God is weaving the great triumphs and terrible tragedies all together for his sovereign purposes in the world, which include changing us. The most dramatic example of this is found at the cross of Christ. Here is where Satan, the Evil One, thought he had won, but God had purposely woven together the actions of sinful men into something that was for our greater good (our salvation). Acts 4 captures it well. After Peter and John were forbidden by the Sanhedrin to preach or teach in the name of Jesus, they reported these things to their people and then prayed aloud in their presence:

Indeed Herod and Pontius Pilate met together with the Gentiles and the people of Israel in this city to conspire against your holy servant Jesus, whom you anointed. They did what your power and will had decided beforehand should happen. (Acts 4:27–28 NIV 1984)

So this is the mystery. Bad things happen, but God works it for good. He already had a plan that Jesus would go to the cross, and evil men put him there. But this was his sovereign purpose, so that we, the ones who are "called according to his purpose," might receive the ultimate good that came even out of the height of human evil.

So we must remember, no matter what happens in life, God is at work behind the scenes, for "He who began a good work in you will carry it on to completion" (Philippians 1:6 NIV 1984).

Even the worst evil that happens to us as Christians is for a greater good (once again—so that God may be glorified, his kingdom purposes advanced, and that we become more like him).

So let's give this a test run, shall we?

A little over fifty years ago, five missionaries from the United States traveled to a remote section of Ecuador to bring the gospel to a notoriously violent tribe known as the Auca Indians. The missionaries were Jim Elliot, Nate Saint, Ed McCully, Roger Youderian, and Peter Fleming, and they began to make contact with these natives from their airplane.

Eventually they set up camp nearby and had a few friendly encounters with some of the natives in an attempt to build a relationship. However, over the course of their interactions a terrible misunderstanding took place and ten of the natives killed all five missionaries with spears and machetes. I'm sure the question at the time was: What good did God have in mind for all this?

Years later, Elisabeth Elliot (the wife of Jim Elliot) and Rachel Saint (the sister of Nate Saint) became further involved in continued missionary efforts to the Auca Indians. Through a young Auca girl named Dayuma, who had run away and been living in exile from the tribe, they were able to learn the language of the Auca Indians, and eventually went back with her to live with Aucas, leading many of them to Christ, even some of the men who earlier had killed their loved ones!

These women seemingly had every right to be grieved and angry over what had happened, yet the grace and love of God compelled them to forgive and to reach out—all in the name of Christ.

So what was the good that God brought from such a terrible tragedy? Simply this: Many Aucas came to saving faith in Christ. The women were used by God to share the gospel and gained a testimony of the power of forgiveness and grace. For the original missionaries who were murdered, their reward was the glory of heaven, and their story inspired hundreds of others to enter the mission field for the cause of Christ.

This is what it means to say that all things work together for good for those that love God and are called according to his purpose. Only God saw the big picture. He was the one who knew his ultimate good plan.

So even if great suffering and tragedy come to your door, please know that as a believer in Christ, God is orchestrating something for his and your good. And as he weaves his plan, we can rejoice in knowing that his plan is tailor-made for each of us as he seeks to make us more like him. Life for the believer may not always feel safe, but it is good (both in this life and in the life to come). There is no greater security than knowing this.

CHAPTER 7

If My People Who Are Called by My Name

"If my people who are called by my name humble themselves, and pray and seek my face and turn from their
wicked ways, then I will hear from heaven and will forgive
their sin and heal their land."

—2 CHRONICLES 7:14

SOMETHING ABOUT biblical archaeology fascinates me. I've
always liked history, and the field of archaeology has the
great privilege of seeing history come to life. Though it can
be arduous work, many researchers say that being on an
archaeological dig is like being a kid in a candy store. There
is no telling when you might come across a piece of history
that tells a story about a people or culture from thousands
of years ago.

The Bible is a book that contains much ancient history. To be sure, it is much more than that. It is the revelation of God to us, and its primary concern is about revealing God and his plan of salvation to us. But even as revelation, its stories and settings are historical in nature, and biblical archaeology has an amazing record of confirming the veracity and historicity of the biblical accounts.

To interpret Scripture correctly, it is not only important to consider the literary context of the passage itself, but to consider its historical context. Much of what took place happened in ancient civilizations, where languages, lifestyles, systems of government, and cultural values varied from age to age and geographical location. The stories in the Bible feature real people, who lived ages ago in cultures very different from ours.

Knowing this history is a key to interpretation, and fortunately, we have an abundance of resources in historical, literary, cultural, and sociological studies that can aid us in our task. Our knowledge base has increased dramatically in this information age, and therefore our ability to understand the historical setting of Scripture is at an all-time high.

One passage of Scripture from the Old Testament is chronically misused because little attention is paid to its historical and cultural context. The verse is 2 Chronicles 7:14, which is often used today in prayer meetings (especially during the annual National Day of Prayer). It is a verse that makes a dramatic promise, and many who love the Lord and love their country have placed their hopes on its truths:

> If my people who are called by my name humble them-
> selves, and pray and seek my face and turn from their

wicked ways, then I will hear from heaven and will forgive their sin and heal their land. (2 Chronicles 7:14)

The verse is riveted with great spiritual truths—the need for humility, prayer, the pursuit of God, and repentance. Furthermore, it promises God's listening ear, forgiveness, and healing. On the surface, it seems to be an ideal verse to claim for believers who long to see righteousness, truth, and blessing fall upon their country. But is it legitimate to use? Let's look at the context.

King David's son Solomon has assumed the role of the king of Israel. He built an incredible temple for the Lord, brought in the ark of the covenant (the symbol of the Lord's presence), and dedicated the temple before the assembled people of God. This becomes a climactic moment for the nation of Israel, as God has fulfilled his promise to David.

As Solomon stands before the people, he delivers a powerful speech, topped by a prayer of dedication. Imagine seeing Solomon kneeling before the Lord, spreading his hands to heaven, and worshiping the Lord by recounting his covenant faithfulness. What a sight!

He prays that the Lord would be attentive to his prayers and the prayers of his people that are offered in this place. He further asks that the Lord would act as judge, the forgiver of sins, and would relent from divine judgment (such as drought and famine) when the people come before him in repentance of their sin.

Solomon asks the Lord to listen to the prayers of foreigners who seek his face at this temple, and that the Lord would bless Israel in time of war. And then finally, if the Lord should allow Israel to be defeated on account of their sin, he asks God to forgive and maintain their cause when they repent. And as he closes his prayer, he appeals to the Lord to definitively act on behalf of this temple, the priests, the people, and himself as the Lord's anointed king.

And in a dramatic visual response in affirmation of Solomon's prayer, fire comes down from heaven and consumes the sacrifices, and the glory of the Lord fills the temple. The people fall down on their faces as they are overwhelmed by this magnificent event and they worship the Lord with singing, sacrifices, and feasts that last for another week. Following this, they return to their homes with joy in their hearts. The glory days of Israel are at an all-time high.

Years pass and Solomon completes his palace as well. Then suddenly, in the middle of the night, the Lord appears to Solomon in private (we are not told how he appears). And what follows is the Lord's personal response to Solomon's very public prayer years before at the temple:

> I have heard your prayer and have chosen this place for myself as a house of sacrifice. When I shut up the heavens so that there is no rain, or command the locust to devour the land, or send pestilence among my people, if my people who are called by my name humble themselves, and pray and seek my face and turn from their wicked ways, then I will hear from heaven and will forgive their sin and heal their land. (2 Chronicles 7:12–14)

There are several things we should note in this passage. This response is specifically given to Solomon, the king who represents and leads God's chosen people, the nation of Israel. The "place" that the Lord is referring to is none other than the temple itself, the "house of sacrifice."

This is significant because the promise that the Lord gives is specifically to *this* king and *these* people in *this* time and *this* place. It is not meant to be a general promise that is given to any other nation on the face of the earth. No other nation could ever claim to be "God's people," and no other nation today has a temple where the living God dwells.

Furthermore, notice that the Lord assumes that Israel (God's people) will sin, for he proclaims that there will be times of drought and famine, where he sends locusts to devour the land and plagues or diseases to inflict the people or livestock, all as an act of judgment for their sin. Yet this judgment will be short-lived if God's people ("who are called by his name") would humble themselves, pray, seek God, and repent.

It is then that the Lord will do an amazing thing in response. Not only will he forgive them for their sin, but he will restore the physical land that was decimated by the physical acts of judgment (drought, locusts, and pestilence). In other words, he will restore the land so that it produces rain again, so that there will be crops and a harvest that will nourish and supply the needs of his people. Again, this particular healing is not necessarily spiritual in nature, but is physical and pertains to the land itself.

The Lord then promises again to hear the prayers offered in the temple and bring continual blessing to Solomon if he remains faithful to walk in accordance with the commands and laws of God.

My hope is that now you can see how this Scripture verse has been plucked from its context and misused. Though the spiritual principles of humility, repentance, prayer, forgiveness, and healing are still relevant for us today, the binding promise of this passage was for another people in another time and another place. It is not a promise for any other nation besides the nation of Israel, those who could rightly be called "God's people."

Furthermore, the healing that is promised is specifically a healing of a physical land, and therefore we can't hijack the idea of healing, generalize it, and apply it as a promise of spiritual revival for any nation where Christians reside. That would be a misuse of the text.

Even so, let me be clear. In no way am I saying that Christians should refuse to pray for their country or their leaders. That would be an act of disobedience. For the apostle Paul, in talking to his protégé Timothy, said:

> First of all, then, I urge that supplications, prayers, intercessions, and thanksgivings be made for all people, for kings and all who are in high positions, that we may lead a peaceful and quiet life, godly and dignified in every way. This is good, and it is pleasing in the sight of God our Savior, who desires all people to be saved and to come to the knowledge of the truth. (1 Timothy 2:1–4)

God is pleased when we pray. He is also pleased when we intercede for others, for our leaders, and for our country. God also desires to see people humble themselves and repent so that they may be saved through faith in Christ and come to the knowledge of the truth. Then they will join the people of God (the church) who are called by his name.

Additionally, they will also find new citizenship in a spiritual kingdom that will stand firm for eternity and cannot be shaken (Hebrews 12:28). They will become citizens of a better country, with a city that has uniquely been prepared for them (Hebrews 11:16). They will be citizens of heaven itself (Philippians 3:20).

Our world is a fallen world, and it does not seem to be getting any better. It will one day pass away. But Christians, take heart in the fact that this world is not our home—heaven is. And one day there will be a new heaven and a new earth. Until that time comes, we should walk faithfully, proclaim the gospel, pray for our country and its leaders, and rejoice in the freedoms that we have the privilege of enjoying.

But we must not mistake the country we live in now for the kingdom of God, even if it is the greatest country on earth, founded on biblical principles, a country still worth living and dying for.

It is a true biblical principle that when people repent, times of refreshing and blessing come (Acts 3:19–20). So in this sense, we should pray that repentance and revival will take hold in our land so that God's forgiveness, grace, and healing would rain down on us. But claiming 2 Chronicles 7:14 as the verse that invokes God's promise and guarantee for this to happen in the exact same way it did to ancient Israel is not an appropriate application.

CHAPTER 8

Jesus As the Firstborn Over All Creation

"He is the image of the invisible God, the firstborn of all creation."

—COLOSSIANS 1:15

THE STORY IS TOLD of a little girl who had quite an imagination. Her name was Jennifer, and she was in her kindergarten class doing what kindergarteners often do. She had taken up her colored pencils and paper for an art assignment and was hard at work creating a masterpiece.

Her teacher walked through the classroom, looking over the students' shoulders, complimenting and encouraging them in their work. But then she came to Jennifer. "Jennifer, sweetheart, what is it that you are trying to draw?"

The precocious five-year-old looked up with complete confidence and said, "I'm drawing God," and then went back to work. A smile came over the teacher's face and she chuckled in her heart; then in all her vast wisdom and knowledge she replied, "But Jennifer, no one knows what God looks like." Without missing a beat, Jennifer kept working and said, "They will in a minute."

In the gospel of John we are told that no one has ever seen the invisible God (in the fullness of his divine glory). To do so would mean instant death due to our inherent sinfulness (Exodus 33:20). But the good news is that God chose to reveal himself in a way that we could handle by becoming flesh and taking on human form (John 1:14, 18; Philippians 2:8). His name is Jesus, and the consistent testimony of the New Testament is that he is fully God made known to us (Philippians 2:6–8; Hebrews 1:1–3).

I don't know about you, but I've always tried to imagine what the people of the first century saw when they met Jesus. As I have traveled in different parts of the world, I've noticed that each culture has its own conception of what Jesus might have looked like. On a recent trip to Japan, I was taken aback when I saw a gospel tract where a cartoon character in the story looked a lot like a Japanese Jesus.

Such is true in parts of Africa and in the West as well. We conceptualize Jesus to look like us. I remember growing up in church looking at a picture of a very Caucasian-looking Jesus with long brown hair and blue eyes praying in the garden of Gethsemane. But the fact is, Jesus was not black or white or Asian looking. He was a Jew from the Middle East.

His skin would have most likely been an olive color, perhaps a tanned look. It is highly probable that he would have had a strong build and a natural, rugged-looking appearance as a man who worked as a carpenter's son for the majority of his life. His hair was most likely short, his face covered with a beard. All of this would have been the common appearance of the majority of Jewish men. Overall, it is quite fair to say that Jesus was likely an average-looking fellow. For even when he was betrayed by Judas, Judas prearranged to point him out to the Roman soldiers by a kiss on the cheek. This may suggest that his appearance did not stand out from the rest, but this is merely speculation.

The bottom line is, the New Testament gives us little description of what Jesus looked like. To be honest, it wasn't really necessary for the apostles to tell us that kind of information. But it *was necessary* to substantiate that Jesus was God in the form of a man (1 John 4:2). His role in being our substitutionary sacrifice (the one who took our place) on the cross depends on this fact.

Yet many false teachers, such as the Gnostics, taught that all physical matter was evil and that only the spirit or non-material things were good. Therefore they asserted that Jesus may have only *appeared* to be human but in actuality he was most likely a ghost or a spirit. Others suggested he was perhaps some kind of celestial angel created by God.

This latter idea (that Jesus was some kind of created angel) is a doctrinal heresy that has been circulated since the days of the early church, but more recently purported by the Jehovah's Witnesses (JWs). According to their false teachings, Jesus was nothing more than the first created angel, the archangel Michael, who was sent from heaven to earth and who became Jesus (a temporary man, and nothing more than a man).

Though he may have been a man while here on earth, JWs teach that upon his death his humanity was completely annihilated and that he was raised from the dead as "an immortal spirit who returned to heaven to once again become the archangel Michael."[1] Furthermore, it was through this created angel (Michael, who became Christ) that God or Jehovah created all other things in the universe. So in their teachings, Jesus may be a "lesser god," but he is not equal to almighty God or Jehovah himself, and he was certainly a created being long before he became a man.[2]

In order to prove their claims, the Jehovah's Witnesses often misuse a verse that on the surface might seem to support their thesis, but upon further investigation fails to substantiate their assertions. The verse is Colossians 1:15:

He is the image of the invisible God, the firstborn of all creation.

The contention of the Jehovah's Witnesses is that the apostle Paul is speaking of Christ as a created being. However, though it is true that *firstborn* usually means the first child born into a family, *this is not what the word means in this particular case,* and the context and surrounding verses make that clear (which we'll see in a moment).

But first, it is important to note that the word *firstborn* can be used in a very different sense. It also may refer to the idea of position, rank, or prominence. Such was the case with King David in the Old Testament, who was the last in the birth order of his family but anointed as "the firstborn, the highest of the kings of the earth" (Psalm 89:27).

Such was also true for the nation of Israel. It is obvious that Israel as a nation was not the first people ever born on the earth (as generations lived before the Lord established the nation). Nevertheless, the Lord told Moses to tell Pharaoh King of Egypt that "Israel is my firstborn son" (Exodus 4:22). In other words, Israel held pride of place as the people whom God had chosen to receive prominence and the inheritance of the Promised Land, and thus "heirs."

This same idea of prominence and rank was also true of Jacob and Esau, whereby Esau was born first, but nevertheless the promised inheritance went to the younger brother Jacob, who was deemed "the firstborn."

All these examples show it is not necessary to conclude that Jesus was a created being merely because he is given the title *firstborn*. Chronology is not always in view. Furthermore, such an interpretation does not make sense due to context. As Paul said in the first part of verse 15, Jesus "is the image of the invisible God." Therefore, he was not "made in the image of God," but rather he *is* the image of God. In other words, he is the likeness of God ("the exact imprint of his nature"—Hebrews 1:3), or none other than God himself.

Additionally, in the next two verses Paul ascribes to Jesus the role of Creator, the one who was "before all things":

> For by him all things were created, in heaven and on earth, visible and invisible, whether thrones or dominions or rulers or authorities—all things were created through him and for him. And he is before all things, and in him all things hold together. (Colossians 1:16–17)

If indeed "all things in *heaven* and earth" were created by Jesus, then it makes no sense to say that Jesus himself was a created being. Furthermore, the fact that Paul says Jesus was "before all things" means that Jesus existed before creation, so he has existed for all eternity. This immediate context refutes the interpretation of the Jehovah's Witnesses that Jesus was a created being. Quite the contrary, Paul is arguing that Jesus is the God who created all things, and that all creation was created through him and for him, and is sustained by him.

The gospel of John also quickly refutes the Jehovah's Witnesses' claim that Jesus is a created being. In John 1:3, the apostle writes:

> All things were made through him, and without him was not any thing made *that was made*.

John says, "All things were made through him." Therefore, Jesus, the second person in the Trinity, could not be regarded as something "that was made," but instead is the Maker himself!

To show how far the Jehovah's Witnesses will go, their own translation of the Bible inserts the word *other* in various places of Colossians 1:15–17, even though the word does not exist in the original Greek text:

> He is the image of the invisible God, the firstborn of all creation; because by means of him all [other] things were created in the heavens and upon the earth, the things visible and the things invisible, no matter whether they are thrones or lordships or governments or authorities. All [other] things have been created through him and for him. Also, he is before all [other] things and by means of him all [other] things were made to exist. (Colossians 1:15–17, *New World Translation* of the Watchtower Society).

By adding the word *other* to their translation, they are seeking to imply that Jesus was first "made" by God and then all "other" things were made by Jesus. This amounts to nothing less than academic dishonesty, because the word *other* neither exists in the original nor is implied by anything else in the context.

This is why I suggested at the beginning of this book that when the Bible is mishandled or used inappropriately (or in this case, mistranslated all for the sake of supporting a theological agenda), it can become a dangerous book.

Anyone who studies photography knows that when the settings on the camera are not properly adjusted, the picture can come out distorted or blurry. Such is also the case when someone interprets the Bible without looking at the context or ignoring what the Bible clearly teaches in other places.

Though we may not have a physical portrait of Jesus, we certainly can discover a proper theological portrait when we interpret Scripture correctly; and what God drew was a masterpiece.

CHAPTER 9

Money Is the Root of All Evil

"For the love of money is a root of all kinds of evils. It is through this craving that some have wandered away from the faith and pierced themselves with many pangs."

—1 TIMOTHY 6:10

MONEY, MONEY, MONEY, money—money! Such are the first words to the top-ten soul hit "For the Love of Money" by the famous R&B group The O'Jays. First popular in the early 1970s, the song has been resurrected and recently used as the musical theme to Donald Trump's reality shows, *The Apprentice* and *The Celebrity Apprentice*.

It's a catchy tune, and Americans love it. The tune, that is. Well . . . maybe the lyrics too.

There's something about money that tends to consume American culture. We happen to be the richest country that has ever existed in the history of the world, for better or for worse. So in looking at one of the more popular misused verses, our attention now turns to money.

There are two things wrong with the title of this chapter, and I've done this on purpose. But first, you should know that the statement "money is the root of all evil" is the one that most people recite when they try to recall what the Bible says about money. The impression (which is clearly false) is that God despises the rich and that money in and of itself is the source of all the evil that exists on this planet. Neither idea is true.

For starters, it would be helpful to recite the entire verse in context and quote the verse with greater accuracy! So let's do that. In my opinion, the best translation of this verse comes out of the English Standard Version, which accurately translates the last phrase in the first sentence of the verse. It reads:

> For the love of money is *a root of all kinds of evils.* It is through this craving that some have wandered away from the faith and pierced themselves with many pangs. (1 Timothy 6:10).

Notice that Paul doesn't denounce money in general per se, but instead he warns us about "the love of money." There is a significant difference here. Nowhere does the Bible teach that it is wrong to possess money or that it is wrong to have large quantities of it. Being rich is not a sin.

However, the Bible does warn us about the many stresses, pressures, and temptations that come with having lots of money, and it instructs us to be responsible, generous, and benevolent, especially to those in need. Furthermore Jesus taught in one of his parables that our possessions (or money) should not possess us (or be our master) in such a way that we become consumed by them and serve them above God. Matthew 6:24 says, "You cannot serve God and money."

What's interesting is that those who have much *and* those who have very little can both be consumed with a passion for money so that it masters them. It is this that Jesus warned against. Only Jesus our Lord should be our master!

So first, the problem rests with the *love* of money, and second, Paul says the love of money is "*a* root of all kinds of evils." Notice the difference here. The popular phrase that people recite usually stems from the King James Version, which reads, "For the love of money is the root of *all* evil" (1 Timothy 6:10 KJV). The KJV seems to suggest that *any and all evil*, irrespective of what it is, has its roots or place of origin in the "love of money." But this does not accurately convey what Paul is saying, and this translation is flawed due to context.

Let me show you what I mean beginning with verse 9. Paul said:

> But those who desire to be rich fall into temptation, into a snare, into many senseless and harmful desires that plunge people into ruin and destruction. (1 Timothy 6:9)

Notice that Paul is talking about the desire to get rich (which many false teachers have) and how easy it is to fall into temptation. This desire or craving for wealth often leads people to embrace senseless and harmful desires that end up ruining lives. In fact, at the end of verse 10, Paul says it is because of this craving that many have wandered away from the faith (the Christian life with all of it spiritual pursuits), and as a result many are self-inflicted with unnecessary hardships, or *griefs,* as the NIV has translated it.

But Paul is not saying that any and all desire is bad, or that all desires lead one's life into ruin, but "many" desires do. So there is a principle here that is working its way through the text. It is not *all* desires, but *many* desires. It is not *all* money per se, but *the love of money;* and it is not *all* evil, but *many kinds* of evils.

Paul is avoiding sweeping statements and generalizations in the context of his argument. Therefore, the better translation that accurately captures the original Greek in its context is this:

For the love of money is a root of all kinds of evils.

This changes the overall picture then. Money itself is not evil, and all the evil that exists is not to be completely tied to money (or even the love of money), though to be fair, much of it can be.

Many have suggested that a major source of human evil is pride—human beings striving to be their own god (which seemingly was Lucifer's temptation as well). This inward bent came as a result of disobeying God and giving in to temptation in the garden of Eden, the place where Eve was tempted to "be like God," or, in essence, to be "her own God." The sin of disobedience that Adam and Eve shared compromised the moral law of God and ushered in the fall of creation, infecting the entire human race.

No matter if it is greed, lust, lies, or any list of vices one might come up with, the sins of humanity are rooted in the cravings of the sinful flesh and the pursuit of one's own glory (in opposition to the glory of God). Though there is such a thing as a healthy self-interest (like self-preservation and the stewardship of one's body), humanity has tragically fallen into a twisted love of self, with an insatiable appetite to please the fallen sin nature to one degree or another.

This, in my mind, is the major root cause of all sin (though the essence of sin itself is lawlessness), and it is an offense to a holy God who alone is worthy of being glorified, worshiped, and obeyed. The only cure for this disease is the transformation and new spiritual life that is received through repentance and faith, believing in Jesus as the One who was crucified and raised from the dead, making full atonement for our sin.

So it is no surprise to hear Jesus say that the essence of discipleship is that each man should "*deny himself* and take up his cross and follow me (Jesus)" (Matthew 16:24). This seems to put things back into their proper order, where obeying God and turning away from the fleshly desire to be your own God is the name of the game.

So it is the love of money—rooted in humanity's pursuit of its own glory—that is the source of tremendous amounts of wickedness. We are repulsed by war, murder, rape, and heinous crimes against humanity, and rightly so, but I believe we should be equally disgusted with the wickedness of individual and corporate greed that has devastated countless lives and is assuredly the root of all kinds of evil.

One final thought. In addition to reading Scripture carefully in context—looking for words, phrases, and ideas before and after the text to help you better understand what the author is truly saying—when someone quotes Scripture, make sure they are quoting it accurately. As we have seen here, the words *the love of* give the oft-recited phrase a completely different meaning.

As I watch political campaigns, I wonder if I am hearing the whole story or a sound bite taken out of context and strategically edited. Inasmuch as this is done in politics, it is also done in religious circles (even by well-meaning people). We would do well then to heed the words that Paul gave to Timothy: "Do your best to present yourself to God as one approved, a worker who has no need to be ashamed, rightly handling the word of truth" (2 Timothy 2:15).

CHAPTER 10

No More
Than You Can Handle

"God is faithful, and he will not let you be tempted beyond
your ability."

—1 CORINTHIANS 10:13

IT'S A COMMENT that's often meant to be a word of encouragement. The road gets rough, and sure enough someone
steps in with good intentions and says, "Remember, God
promised he would never give us more than we can handle."
But somehow that doesn't always lighten the load. In fact,
it is fair to question if it's even true, and secondly, where it's
found!

The apostle Paul had a lot of difficult times. As a pioneer
missionary who often traveled into hostile territory, he spoke
readily about his sufferings for Christ. Paul used some pretty

hefty words in 2 Corinthians 6 to describe the seriousness of this suffering: afflictions, hardships, distresses, beatings, imprisonment, hard work, sleepless nights, hunger, sorrow, mistreatment, having nothing, and so on (see 2 Corinthians 6:4–10).

Was it more than he could handle? Listen to what Paul says at the beginning of this very same letter:

> For we do not want you to be unaware, brothers, of the affliction we experienced in Asia. For we were so utterly burdened beyond our strength that we despaired of life itself. Indeed, we felt that we had received the sentence of death. (2 Corinthians 1:8–9)

It sure sounds like God gave Paul more than he could handle. His personal strength was sapped, and he fell into despair such that he wanted to die. But why? Why would God do that? All we have to do is read on and finish out the rest of verse 9.

> . . . But that was to make us rely not on ourselves but on God who raises the dead. (2 Corinthians 1:9)

Ah, so this is why God allowed Paul to be "burdened beyond his strength." The Lord was teaching Paul not to rely upon his own strength but rather to rely upon the strength that comes from God—the same strength and power God exerted when he raised Christ from the dead (Ephesians 1:19–20).

So the popular notion that "God will never give us more than we can handle" is in reality a blatant falsehood—a lie. He *will* give us more than we can handle, and this for the express purpose of bringing us to the end of ourselves so that we realize our very life, breath, and sustaining power comes only from God all the time. Jesus clearly said, "Apart from me you can do *nothing*" (John 15:5).

So where does this well-intentioned idea come from anyway? My suspicion is that it is a spin-off of what Paul said in 1 Corinthians 10:13:

No temptation has overtaken you that is not common to man. God is faithful, and he will not let you be tempted beyond your ability, but with the temptation he will also provide the way of escape, that you may be able to endure it. (1 Corinthians 10:13)

If you look closer at the text, it has a specific nuance that is worthy of note. Paul is not talking about the general circumstances and hardships of life. He is talking specifically about *temptation*.

The setting is this. Paul is warning the Corinthian Christians about the dangers of being arrogant and overly confident in their ability to resist temptation. Before they came to faith in Christ, many of the Corinthians worshiped idols. They attended popular feasts and festivals that were celebrated in the temples of pagan gods. They ate and drank to excess, and participated in all the revelry and immorality that was a part of Corinth's social world.

Now that they were Christians, they no longer worshiped idols, but they apparently still wanted to be a part of the city's social life. So they began to rationalize. They felt that as long as they had the proper perspective on idols, the idols were in fact meaningless. They could give themselves the absolute freedom to participate in these social activities so long as they didn't succumb to temptation. This, however, was like playing with fire, and Paul knew it. First Corinthians 8–10 was his answer to their "freedom in Christ."

Paul first delivered a stern warning that even though they did indeed have freedom in Christ, they must be very careful with it and not use it as a license that could somehow cause someone else to fall into sin. It would not be a good idea to exercise that freedom in front of other Christians who were not strong enough to resist temptation. That would be extremely unloving and selfish, and therefore Paul wanted them to be willing to limit their freedom for the sake of the "weaker brethren."

Then he uses his own life as an example of self-limitation for the sake of others. Paul often renounced his own rights and freedoms for the sake of the gospel. For example, even though he had every right as an apostle to receive financial support from the church (1 Corinthians 9:14), he nevertheless forsook that right and worked bi-vocationally as a tentmaker just to avoid the criticism of some of the Corinthians who may have felt that he was only preaching for money.

So Paul limited his freedom and the exercise of his own rights in order to prevent his ministry from being misunderstood and criticized (and there were other reasons as well), and he did this all to win more people to Christ. Anyone who has been a missionary or has gone on short-term missions trips knows that there are times when you may have to limit your own freedoms for the sake of winning over the hearts of your intended audience who have many cultural restrictions and convictions of their own. That's what Paul did.

But the Corinthians were not like Paul. They were a little puffed up and not so careful. They were willing to push their freedom to extremes and flirt with disaster because they thought they were "mature" enough to resist the temptation to fall back into their old ways.

After using some Old Testament illustrations about how Israel constantly fell into temptation, Paul warns the Corinthians about having overconfidence in their own ability to resist it, and tells them they should "take heed lest [they] fall" (1 Corinthians 10:12).

But then Paul turns the corner and talks about temptation in general. He goes from a warning to a word of encouragement and insight. And this is where our verse comes in. He begins by talking about the normal human experience and commonality of temptation that everyone endures from time to time. In other words, we all face it, without exception. No one should ever say, "Well, my temptation is different, and no one else has ever been tempted quite like this." One writer has correctly pointed out: "Circumstances differ but basic temptations do not."[1]

Temptation is a universal experience. And as a side note, please know that it is not wrong to be tempted, but it is wrong to give in to it. But Paul gives us some good news. We don't have to give in to temptation, because God will always supply a way out of it. Again, Paul says:

God is faithful, and he will not let you be tempted beyond your ability, but with the temptation he will also provide the way of escape, that you may be able to endure it. (1 Corinthians 10:13)

So here is where God will not allow you to have more than you can handle. It is with respect to *temptation*. Paul pictures God looking into your situation and sympathizing with it, extending a hand to help get you out (see also Hebrews 4:15).

Therefore, no one should ever say that they had no choice but to sin because the temptation was too great and there was no way to escape it.

God knows a person's limits with regard to temptation, and he will not allow any temptation to supersede a person's ability to resist it. He will provide the spiritual resources necessary for us to sufficiently endure it. Furthermore, when we are tempted, we should also be looking for the God-ordained way out of it. When the smoke of temptation is thick and the fire is raging, we should be looking for the clearly marked exit signs that lead us to fresh air and safety.

The writer of Hebrews reminds us that Jesus is our aid in this:

> For because he himself has suffered when tempted, he is able to help those who are being tempted. (Hebrews 2:18)

In other words, we have an advocate and a helper in Jesus Christ, who opens the door of escape for us. Taking cues from Jesus' own temptations in the wilderness, our best weapon against temptation is none other than the Word of God itself—or as Paul calls it, "the sword of the Spirit" (Ephesians 6:17). Each time Satan went after Jesus and attacked him head-on, Jesus remembered and recited a verse and with that weapon resisted the onslaught and sharp arrows of the Adversary.

This is why it is so important to memorize Scripture. The "ability to endure" has everything to do with how well our souls have been shaped and fortified by the Word of God. It should reside deep within us. It has been the experience of many Christians (including myself) that the Spirit of God has a way of bringing Scripture to mind at just the right moment whenever temptation arrives on the scene. What a gift of God! It is a source of power that enables us to stand firm (along with prayer—Mark 14:38).

What Paul is saying then is good news for us. This is the area where God will not allow us to be broadsided with more than we can handle—temptation. But when it comes to life's hardships and difficulties, we should be prepared to receive more than we can handle so that we learn to rely on God and not ourselves. Either way, whether it is in great trials or in moments of great temptation, looking to and leaning on God is the answer. He is faithful.

CHAPTER 11

Train Up a Child

"Train up a child in the way he should go; even when he is old he will not depart from it."

—PROVERBS 22:6

NO ONE EVER SAID being a parent is easy. Still, when my wife and I had our first child, I remember thinking, "Okay, how hard could this be? We feed him, change his diapers, and put him down for naps, and after he grows a little things will get easier." It was a rather naïve view, to say the least, and it didn't take long before my imaginary world received a heavy dose of reality.

As a father of two very active boys, I can honestly say that being a parent is one of the greatest blessings of my life. The joy they bring to my wife and me is so profound that, to be honest, we're not sure what we did in the eight years of marriage before we had them. We can't imagine life without them, and the lessons we learn each day remind us they are truly gifts from God.

But again, this doesn't mean it's easy. Parenting requires patience, humility, and sacrifice. I'm also convinced that it is one of the divinely ordained ways that God works on our sanctification, especially when it comes to the idea of servant-hood. In the first few months of being a parent, I genuinely learned how selfish I really am and what it means to serve. My agenda and my schedule had to take a backseat to the immediate needs of the moment (feedings, diaper changes, etc.). This was good medicine for me, and it reminds a person that life is not all about them.

Those initial years of parenting also caused us to seek out wise counsel and instruction on how to raise a child accord-ing to biblical principles. Mutually agreeing on how to build up, train, and discipline our children in both a formative and corrective sense continues to be an ongoing conversation even to this day, as it should.

Early on, we read many books about Christian parenting, and some were better than others. But none can ever replace the primary source of wisdom for raising children: the Bible. The Bible has much to say about the responsibilities of parents as the primary faith influencers of their children.

Now, it is certainly true that a major way for a parent to influence a child is simply by example, by loving the Lord with all your heart and living a faithful life in front of them. For children are imitators of what they see. But one of the greatest ways that parents can influence their children is by intentionally teaching them the Scriptures, or as God says in Deuteronomy, impressing the commands of God on them by talking about spiritual truths "when you sit at home and when you walk along the road, when you lie down and when you get up" (Deuteronomy 6:7 NIV 1984).

The Bible is full of helpful, practical advice on what to do and what not to do in raising children. We are warned about the dangers of withholding discipline, and yet we are also cautioned not to be overly strict and cause them to become resentful or filled with despair.

Truth be told, there is no such thing as a perfect parent. We are all sinners and we all make mistakes. But the important thing is that we create a culture of grace in our homes, where healthy communication, biblical principles, and spiritual formation become staples of everyday life.

One biblical principle that is often misunderstood for an absolute promise is found in Proverbs 22:6. It is a well-known verse that parents of older children often cling to when they watch their children go through times of rebellion or struggle:

> Train up a child in the way he should go; even when he is old he will not depart from it. (Proverbs 22:6)

As a pastor, I recall many a time when parents approached me with that desperate look in their eyes as they attempted to grapple with the significance of this verse for a child who had gone astray. It is a heartbreaking experience to watch your son or daughter abandon the way of life that was modeled and taught to them as they grew up in a God-fearing home. No one knows why it happens, but somehow they must come to grips with what they believe on their own, and part of that process may unfortunately involve a difficult season of poor decisions and painful consequences.

In the early 1990s I had an opportunity to serve in Christian ministry at a secular college campus in Ohio, and it was interesting to watch the incoming freshmen who had been raised in Christian homes. Some remained faithful to their family upbringing and others did not. Either way, each student had to ask the natural questions: "Is this faith I was raised in really mine? Do I own and believe these truths for myself or am I merely a product of an environment that had a belief system that I have never really embraced?"

Those who embraced faith in Christ seemed to grow spiritually rather fast during those formative college years, but those who rejected their Christian heritage quickly succumbed to "college life" and went in the wrong direction, revealing the true condition of their hearts. And when that happens, many Christian parents find themselves distraught because they feel helpless and unable to do anything about it.

I can only imagine how the father felt in the biblical story of the prodigal, watching his son walk away. It must have been gut-wrenching. Many parents today who see their sons and daughters rebel feel the same way. But if they come back, like the prodigal son did in the story, there is profound rejoicing.

All of this forces us to examine Proverbs 22:6. At first glance it seems to indicate that if a child who was raised well falls into rebellion, it is only a matter of time before they are guaranteed to return to what is right. But this misses the nature of a proverb.

Others interpret it differently, saying that training a child "in the way he should go" merely means to train him or her according to their natural bent and tendencies (e.g., "strong-willed" or "insecure"). When understood this way, it would therefore communicate that we should train them according to their own predisposed path. But this understanding does not match the overall themes of the book.

The book of Proverbs makes it clear that there is a "right path" and a "wrong path," and one is the way of the wise and the other is the way of the fool. The "right path" requires the parent to exercise much hard work, training, and discipline in order to train the child to walk in it. And the reason this is a lot of work is because the child's natural tendencies are usually of the flesh due to the inherent sin nature that we are all born with. As one commentator has rightly noted, "It is hard to explain why a natural bent needs training."[1]

So with this in mind, it is not likely that the proverb was intended to advise us to train our children according to their natural bent. Though it is true that we must be cognizant of our child's unique personality and adapt our parental approaches accordingly, this is not what this proverb is aiming toward.

So what is it saying? Does it intend to communicate that raising a child in the "right path" is an absolute guarantee that he or she will always come back to it no matter what kind of temporary rebellion may take place? Not necessarily. But to understand why this is not a guarantee, one has to understand the nature of the book of Proverbs. *Most proverbs are principles, not promises.* They are general insights and truisms based on observation and experience, but they are not meant to be universal guarantees that will come to pass 100 percent of the time.

The goal of this proverb is to admonish us to train our children, especially in the "way of wisdom," which is the proper "way he should go." This is none other than "God's" path, the way of righteousness. Therefore, the proverb suggests that as a matter of historical observation, when this kind of training is consistently done, it usually brings positive results, especially when the child grows older and comes of age.

I'm sure you would agree with me that who we are today has much to do with how we were raised and taught in our early formative years. Children are easily influenced. Let me give you a simple example.

There was a time when we thought it would be fun to let our two boys watch the classic cartoon *Tom and Jerry*, where the rivalry between the cat and the mouse often ends up in some rather hilarious comical roughhousing. The creativity of the show is marvelous as these two rambunctious characters go at each other with full force. We laughed together, and the belly laughs of our boys sure brightened the room.

But when the show was over, we were in for a surprise. The level of energy and creativity that our boys took from that show resulted in all kinds of crying episodes. It didn't take long to realize our kids were not quite ready for *Tom and Jerry* because they could not yet draw the line between playacting and reality. No matter what Hollywood says, movies shape us and are not merely reflections of what is already taking place in our culture.

The writer of Proverbs is stating a longstanding general principle about raising children that is just as true today as it was back then. Hearts and minds are shaped at an early age, and children imitate what they see. So when godly parents create a culture at home where they exercise healthy, formative, and corrective discipline on their children, it will most likely result in healthy thinking and behaviors as they grow older. Again, this is not a hard-and-fast promise but a general principle that stems out of years of observation and experience.

The Old Testament scholar Tremper Longman III provides some excellent closing remarks and a warning when it comes to understanding Proverbs 22:6. He writes:

> The point is that this proverb encourages parents to train their children, but does not guarantee that if they do so their children will never stray. This insight into the form of the proverb is particularly important for parents to grasp when their adult children have not turned out well; otherwise, the verse becomes a sledgehammer of guilt—a purpose that it was not intended to carry. On the other side, the proverb should not become a reason for pride if one's children turn out well either. The proverb is simply an encouragement to do the right thing when it comes to raising one's children.[2]

If you're a parent, don't lose hope. Keep modeling the faith. Even if your children are grown up and out of the house such that your daily influence is minimal, keep walking faithfully. And if at some point you failed in the past, admit it (even to your children) and make a vow to change. Children still see into the hearts of their parents, no matter how old they are.

CHAPTER 12

I Can Do All Things

"I can do all things through Christ who strengthens me."
—Philippians 4:13 NKJV

IMAGINE TWO BOYS playing on opposing basketball teams. They don't know each other, but they have something in common. They're both from healthy Christian homes where they've been taught to love and serve God. Each also knows a little about the Bible. In fact, they love the same Bible verse, one of the first each committed to memory, Philippians 4:13:

I can do all things through Christ who strengthens me. (NKJV)

The basketball game proves to be a fierce competition. For four quarters the boys run, jump, shoot, and rebound as hard as they can, both fortified by the thought *I can do all things through Christ who strengthens me.* But at the end of the day, only one kid and his team will be a winner. And on the way home, they'll each stare out their car window and have two completely different thoughts.

One will tell himself, *You know, God is awesome—he really does give me strength. We won. What an awesome game.* The other is thinking quite the opposite: *Where was God when I needed him today? I guess his strength is not as strong as I thought. What a joke.*

So what do we do? Which boy is right? How does the promise of Philippians 4:13 work for us?

Say I'm carrying a heavy bag of water softener salt into the house from the trunk of my car. Is it legitimate to say to myself, *I can do all things through Christ who gives me strength*? If I drop it, does that make me weak, or was it God's fault because he didn't give me enough strength? Surely that's not what Paul means here.

Again, when we take Scripture out of context and try to use the Bible how we see fit, we can easily set ourselves up for defeat. In fact, we can become so disillusioned with God that we practically shipwreck our faith because he's not meeting our expectations. *God said he would do this, and he's not!* Next thing you know, we begin to doubt the Bible's integrity and ultimately God's ability to do what he promises.

So the question is: What is Paul really saying to us in Philippians 4:13? How should this truth apply to our lives? Are we talking about physical strength, spiritual strength, emotional strength, or a combination of all of them?

Furthermore, what does "all things" mean? Should a bank robber rightfully tell himself, *I can do all things through Christ who gives me strength* the moment he grabs that stack of money? That's silly, of course, but it does reflect how some people handle Scripture. Certainly the idea of being able to do "all things" needs to be qualified. So let's get to work and do a little digging, because I believe the real message Paul is giving here is something we all need to grasp.

The New Testament book of Philippians was written by the apostle Paul while he was under house arrest in Rome. Facing an uncertain future, Paul was not sure whether he would be executed by the Romans, who were widely known for persecuting the church. Still, he felt compelled to write a letter to the first church he started in Greece, in the region of Macedonia. The church was in the city of Philippi, which existed until about the middle of the thirteenth century AD.

According to the New Testament, the first convert to Christ in Philippi was a woman named Lydia (Acts 16:14–15). Not long after this success, Paul and his ministry colleague Silas were imprisoned in Philippi for "interfering" with local commerce by casting demons out of a slave girl who was making money for her owners as a fortune-teller. Even in prison, though, they led a Philippian jailer to faith in Christ.

Under Paul's influence, the church in Philippi grew and became relatively healthy. The church would often send him financial support while he was out on the mission field, and part of Paul's reason for writing this letter was to thank them for their support.

But more than anything, Paul's letter to the Philippians is meant to be a word of update, encouragement, and exhortation. Paul desires to see them grow spiritually and to serve God faithfully without any attachment to the world. He wants them to be unified, experiencing the joy that is found in Christ. In fact, the words *joy* and *rejoice* are used no less than sixteen times in the book's four chapters.

This was obviously something the Philippians struggled with. They loved the Lord but had put a lot of confidence in their own ability to live out the Christian life. As a result, they were getting worried, agitated, and seemingly irritated with each other.

Little has changed for us today. It is easy to become consumed by worry. *Where are we going to get the money? Where can I find the time to get all this done? How's this going to work out?* These types of worries can quickly hijack our faith and keep us from serving the Lord (see Jesus' teaching in Mark 4:19). The truth is, when we are wrapped up in worldly things and distracted by our circumstances, it hinders our spiritual growth and squelches our usefulness in God's kingdom.

Are *you* worried about your needs? Do you wonder how God will provide, especially if you do not see a way? I assure you that you're not alone. All of us face similar fears from time to time. So for a minute, let's pretend we are members of the Philippian church and let Paul's words minister to us.

Paul's desire was to see the church standing firm in the faith. He urged them to be quick to reconcile strained relationships, always rejoice in the Lord, refuse to be anxious, pray about everything, and fix their minds on the things that are excellent and praiseworthy. To the very end of the letter, his aim was to encourage them not to worry about their needs:

God will meet all your needs according to his glorious riches in Christ Jesus. (Philippians 4:19 NIV 1984)

God *was* there. He had not left the Philippians. He knew their situation and he knew their needs. And as the apostle Peter taught us well in the Gospels from his experience with Jesus: If you spend more time fearing the wind and the waves instead of keeping your eyes on Christ, you are bound to find yourself sinking fast with a faltering faith (see Matthew 14:22–31).

To be sure, living by faith is not always easy. But it is what God requires of us. He never promised us an easy life. Furthermore, he doesn't want us to be too comfortable. There is so much more to look forward to in the future life to come. So the bottom line is this: We have to trust God, knowing that he has promised to meet our needs (see Matthew 6:25–34). Anything less than that is dishonoring to God, because it is not his will that our hearts be in turmoil or gripped with worry.

Although Paul reminds the Philippians that God always provides for his people, and even uses their gifts to Paul as an example, he also lets them in on a little secret, a pearl of wisdom we often overlook. It is God's gift of contentment—learning to be content no matter the circumstances:

> I rejoice greatly in the Lord that at last you have renewed your concern for me. Indeed, you have been concerned, but you had no opportunity to show it. I am not saying this because I am in need, for I have learned to be content whatever the circumstances. I know what it is to be in need, and I know what it is to have plenty. I have learned the secret of being content in any and every situation, whether well fed or hungry, whether living in plenty or in want. (Philippians 4:10–12 NIV 1984)

So yes, Paul received their gift and was profoundly grateful. But he uses this teachable moment to share with them a binding principle that should be the norm for every Christian: *No matter what your situation is in life, learn to be content—* whether well fed or hungry, rich or poor, and so on. And our ability to be content in the midst of human struggles is due to this one poignant truth: I can do everything through him who gives me strength.

Aha! So here is the real context for this verse. Paul is talking about contentment. It's as if he's saying, "I have learned to be content in any and every situation because God is the One who is giving me the spiritual strength to be content." God had given him the power not to worry.

Sign me up, right? Oh, how life might be different if we tapped in to the spiritual strength that God provides so that we could quit worrying about our needs and find a real and lasting sense of contentment. No doubt we'd worry less and rejoice more. Perhaps a deeper sense of peace would guard our lives. We'd be less irritable, more optimistic, and focused on spiritual matters. I would venture that even our times of prayer and worship would be much sweeter.

What a joy it would be to come to the place in our lives where we knew that we could trust in Christ to provide and rest in his strength for any and "all things." To have that kind of spiritual strength would be amazing. Monumental. And according to what Paul says, absolutely possible.

So Philippians 4:13 is not so much about having the strength to stand up and sing a solo in church. It's not really about who has the strength to play to the best of their abilities in a sporting contest, or about having the strength to lift a bag of salt. And it certainly isn't about having the courage and strength to rob a bank!

This verse is about having the strength to be content when we are facing those moments in life when physical resources are minimal. This is about having faith in the God who provides—the God who is sovereignly in control over every circumstance in life, the God who sees and knows our needs and has promised to meet them in Christ!

Please understand that even Paul the apostle had to learn this. For example, Paul told the Corinthian church about a time when he was pleading with God to remove something from his life ("a thorn") that was causing him to be incredibly weak. It was perhaps a physical struggle of some kind, but we don't know for sure. Either way, something was causing him pain, and he desired relief. But God chose not to change his circumstance. Instead, he gave Paul strength to face his weakness:

> But [the Lord] said to me, "My grace is sufficient for you, for my power is made perfect in weakness." Therefore I will boast all the more gladly about my weaknesses, so that Christ's power may rest on me. That is why, for Christ's sake, I delight in weaknesses, in insults, in hardships, in persecutions, in difficulties. For when I am weak, then I am strong. (2 Corinthians 12:9–10 NIV 1984)

This perfectly illustrates the truth Paul was also trying to teach the Philippians: God provides the strength and power to be content when life is not ideal; he gives us the necessary grace to persevere and overcome. Furthermore, there was something about being weak that gave God's power an opportunity to be put on display, and in the end this brought glory to God. And since this was Paul's ultimate goal anyway (to showcase God and bring him glory), he took delight in the grace of God that gave him the spiritual strength to be content.

It's tempting to think, *When I get a raise, I will be settled and secure,* or *As soon as I get married I'll find contentment at last*. But these sorts of things are smoke screens for the believer in Christ. Paul didn't have a house. He didn't have a car. He didn't have a big wardrobe or a closet full of shoes. He didn't have degrees on his wall or citations pinned to his chest. He didn't have friends to fellowship with all the time or a wife to comfort him when he was sad.

All in all, Paul traveled pretty light. He had a few clothes, maybe some writing instruments, a few scrolls of the Bible, some paper (or papyrus) to write on. Not much more than that. And yet Paul was content. What a lesson for you and me.

So yes, Philippians 4:13 is a very powerful verse, especially when it is rightly understood and rightly applied. Remember that you can be content and find the physical strength to endure all things, because it is Christ who strengthens you. And when we are content to rely upon him, he is truly glorified, because his strength is on display.

CHAPTER 13

An Eye for an Eye

"If there is serious injury, you are to take life for life, eye for eye, tooth for tooth, hand for hand, foot for foot, burn for burn, wound for wound, bruise for bruise."

—Exodus 21:23–25 NIV 1984

ONE OF MY FAVORITE MOVIES is the 1987 comedy *The Princess Bride*. I consider it one of the greatest comedies of all time. The cast of characters, the blistering one-liners, the crazy plot—they're all part of a masterfully created movie that has drawn almost a cult following. Dedicated fans have a way of randomly finding each other in public, and it usually begins by simply quoting a line from the movie. Ears perk up, a smile ensues, and a soul connection is made.

One plotline involves the actor Mandy Patinkin playing the role of Inigo Montoya, a Spanish swordsman who is on a personal mission to avenge the death of his beloved father. His father was a sword maker, and when Inigo was a small boy, his father was ruthlessly murdered by a man with six fingers on his right hand in what was essentially a business deal gone bad.

When the boy rose up with his father's sword to fight his father's killer, the killer laughed at the boy and put scars on his face to warn him that his bravery would do nothing but get him killed. Inigo was indeed scarred for life, in more ways than one, and he vowed that as he grew older he would seek revenge and dedicate his life to studying fencing in order to one day bring justice to his father's killer.

Inigo's search for the "six-fingered man" became a lifelong quest, and at some point he decided that when he found him, he would first address him with these now-famous words that he had clearly memorized: "Hello. My name is Inigo Montoya. You killed my father. Prepare to die."

We hear this line repeated by Inigo over and again, especially in the battle that ensues when he successfully finds and engages the killer. As the fight rages on, Inigo repeats his crisply prepared formal greeting with all the gusto he can muster until finally his thirst for revenge is quenched and the battle is over, and the "six-fingered man" is no more.

As the movie comes to a close, Inigo seems relieved but also perplexed. He tells his friend Westley, "It's very strange. I have been in the revenge business so long, now that it's over, I don't know what to do with the rest of my life."

What a problem, wouldn't you agree? I realize it's merely a movie, and it's meant to be funny, but sadly, it's not that far from real life. There are people today who are bent on getting revenge for perceived injustices they have suffered.

Though God clearly says, "Vengeance is mine, I will repay" (Deuteronomy 32:35; Romans 12:19; Hebrews 10:30), this is often ignored or overlooked by those who have personal vendettas or by those who simply can't wait for justice to be done. They are tempted to take matters in their own hands, and even though God has clearly established governing authorities on the earth to restrain evil and to dispense justice in criminal cases (Romans 13), many refuse to wait for this process to come to fruition. These end up being some of the more serious cases of revenge that sometimes make the newspapers.

Yet even in those cases that are not newsworthy, when someone feels wronged or has been hurt, there is often a temptation to retaliate in some way instead of deciding to forgive or "turn the other cheek," as Jesus taught. And oftentimes a biblical citation that is used to justify retaliation is found in such places as Exodus 21:24, Leviticus 24:20, and Deuteronomy 19:21, which all mention "eye for eye, tooth for tooth." It is a common phrase that is selectively quoted out of context, and it was even misunderstood and misused in Jesus' day.

Many people feel that it serves as a license for someone to do equal harm to someone else who has harmed them. For example, if you hit my arm, I'll hit your arm, or if you dent my car, I'll break your windshield. Even if the initial harm done was by accident, some individuals feel perfectly justified in settling the score, so to speak, and may appeal to this verse.

But to understand God's true intention when he commanded "eye for eye," we need to go back to the original context, and for our purposes we will go to its first occurrence in Exodus 21. Here is where we find the laws that God gave to Moses as a means of governing the nation of Israel upon their freedom and release from the hand of the pharaoh in Egypt.

Within the pages of these laws, God defines different crimes and commands particular punishments. Yet knowing the sin nature of human beings, God also sought to protect individuals from excessive punishment when such justice was to be delivered. Putting it into today's terms, God was concerned that the punishment must fit the crime.

For example, it would be an abuse of justice if someone was given twenty years in prison for going ten miles over the speed limit. First off, we'd all be in prison. But second, the punishment doesn't fit the crime. Therefore, in order to avoid this type of injustice, God made it clear that the punishment could never exceed the damage done, and thus the phrase *eye for eye*.

It would do us well to look at the wider context, because within this passage there are some other interesting details. The text falls into a section of laws regarding violence, and the relevant paragraph is found in Exodus 21:22–25:

> If men who are fighting hit a pregnant woman and she gives birth prematurely but there is no serious injury, the offender must be fined whatever the woman's husband demands and the court allows. But if there is serious injury, you are to take life for life, eye for eye, tooth for tooth, hand for hand, foot for foot, burn for burn, wound for wound, bruise for bruise. (NIV 1984)

It's a rather interesting scenario to be sure—spelling out the appropriate punishment if a pregnant woman or her baby is harmed by two men fighting. Today we call this the principle of *lex taliones*, a Latin phrase from the sixteenth century that essentially sets forth the laws concerning retaliation.

Yet in this law given to Moses, depending on the circumstance, it seems clear that the death penalty was not out of the question in cases where the brawl was serious enough to cause the death of either the woman or her child.[1] Interestingly, the Bible is ascribing personhood to the unborn child that was forced to be born prematurely, which ought to teach us that any developing unborn baby has equal value when compared to the life of an adult.

When we come to the New Testament, Jesus addresses this principle and affirms its legitimacy as a means to limiting punishment, but he was also concerned about the similar kind of misuse of this verse that is still happening today. It was never meant to be a so-called proof text to legitimize personal vengeance within interpersonal relationships. This verse was primarily meant to guide the judges and the courts.

In an effort to correct the misuse of the verse, Jesus sets forth a significant new way of thinking and relating for anyone who is tempted to use this as grounds for personal retaliation:

> You have heard that it was said, "An eye for an eye and a tooth for a tooth." But I say to you, Do not resist the one who is evil. But if anyone slaps you on the right cheek, turn to him the other also. And if anyone would sue you and take your tunic, let him have your cloak as well. And if anyone forces you to go one mile, go with him two miles. Give to the one who begs from you, and do not refuse the one who would borrow from you. (Matthew 5:38–42)

In essence, Jesus is encouraging the offended party to back down when wronged and is even suggesting that he or she give up their "right" to resist or fight back when offended. In other words, leave the justice to the courts, and in the context of the personal relationship, be willing to forgive and turn the other cheek. In fact, Jesus is suggesting that even in the face of being wronged a person should seek to respond with a gracious, benevolent generosity: "If he takes your tunic, let him have your cloak as well."

So if someone insults you, not only should you not insult them back, you should seek to reply with uncharacteristic kindness. Such is the manner of love that should be a trait of those who follow Christ. It is nothing short of an imitation of the Savior, who loved us "even while we were yet sinners" (Romans 5:8).

The apostle Paul further capitulated and summarized this teaching by Christ when he instructed the church in Rome in a similar fashion:

> Beloved, never avenge yourselves, but leave it to the wrath of God, for it is written, "Vengeance is mine, I will repay, says the Lord." To the contrary, "if your enemy is hungry, feed him; if he is thirsty, give him something to drink; for by so doing you will heap burning coals on his head." Do not be overcome by evil, but overcome evil with good. (Romans 12:19–21)

This, then, rightly sheds light on the biblical teaching concerning retaliation. As Christians, whenever we are wronged, we should allow for the courts to do their job, and with respect to the personal aspects of it, we should seek to respond in a Christlike manner.

CHAPTER 14

The Prayer Offered
in Faith

"The prayer offered in faith will make the sick person well."

—JAMES 5:15 NIV 1984

IT WAS THE FALL of 1993, and I had entered my first year of
seminary. I had recently graduated from college and was
invited to serve on the pastoral staff of an exciting new church
planted on a thriving campus of a private, liberal arts uni-
versity. This season of life was exciting, filled with spiritual
growth, challenge, and promise.

My faith to this point had never faced any major tests. To
be fair, there was the occasional "mini-crisis" along the way,
but I had gone through life relatively unscathed. That was
about to change.

During the seminary's fall break, I returned to my family homestead in Indiana to celebrate my birthday with my father since our birthdays were so close—mine on October 19 and his on October 20. There was always something special about being able to celebrate my birthday with my dad (and ironically, my younger son was also born on October 19).

At the time, my father had been struggling physically. Seven years prior, he had suffered a massive heart attack and had quadruple bypass surgery, all of which left his heart relatively weak. The years following were rough for him, and he became a candidate for a heart transplant. So, when I returned home for a visit that fall, there was a spirit of urgency and optimism in the air over the possibility that he could receive a new heart at any moment.

Being a man of faith, my father knew that the uncertainty that lay in front of him was not to be faced alone. He deeply wanted to experience God's presence, and prayed often for blessing and healing in his life. He longed for the prayers of others as well. So while I was home, Dad decided to call the leadership of our little country church to come over to our house so they could pray over him and anoint him with oil in keeping with the practice of the early church in James 5:13–16:

> Is any one of you in trouble? He should pray. Is anyone happy? Let him sing songs of praise. Is any one of you sick? He should call the elders of the church to pray over him and anoint him with oil in the name of the Lord. And the prayer offered in faith will make the sick person well; the Lord will raise him up. If he has sinned, he will be forgiven. Therefore confess your sins to each other and pray for each other so that you may be healed. The prayer of a righteous man is powerful and effective. (NIV 1984)

Sounds simple, doesn't it? Dad was facing an uncertain future and wanted God to strengthen him spiritually and perhaps, if it was the Lord's will, to heal him physically. So applying this verse to his situation was the most logical thing for him to do.

It wasn't long before Charles Balsbaugh, a godly older gentleman from our church, pulled up to our driveway in his grain truck. I was puzzled, though, when no one else came. *Didn't the text say elders (plural)?*

To my surprise, my father had it in his mind to affirm me in an unexpected way. He turned to Charles and said, "Charles, I would like my own son to anoint me since he is now a pastor, if that is okay with you."

Immediately my heart raced, because this would be the first time doing this since recently assuming the role of a pastor. I had seen it before, so I knew what to do. But I would have never guessed that I would be anointing my own father. It was a privilege beyond measure, and I was a little nervous. Nevertheless, we found some olive oil from the kitchen, I grabbed my Bible, and my father sat in a chair in the living room while I read the passage directly from the book of James.

As I stood in front of him and read, I could see his eyes looking up at me. In many ways I felt as if my father was implicitly communicating his approval on my life and sense of calling by asking me to do this. And after a time of confession, I then took some oil and anointed his forehead. Charles and I then laid our hands on his shoulders and prayed for his spiritual strength and potential healing right then and there.

Three days later, my father was dead.

When I returned to seminary a couple of days after we prayed over him, all seemed well. However, that Saturday morning, my father's heart suddenly went out of rhythm. He was taken by ambulance to the nearest hospital and rushed into the ER. But after working on him, his heart apparently stopped and was too weak to be restarted. He was fifty-four.

I was in total disbelief when I got the call saying he had passed. He had looked great when I was home. We had a wonderful time together and were greatly looking forward to the possibility of a heart transplant. Moreover, we had anointed him and prayed for God to bring healing to his body. *How could this be? What did we do wrong?*

Eventually, this led me to come to terms with the teaching of James 5. I knew my father was promoted to glory (and in that sense I didn't want him back), but why didn't the Lord heal my father in keeping with the promise? Was I misunderstanding this? We'd prayed in faith. We'd followed the Scriptures. Why did God take him away from us only a few days later? This was not only a family crisis, but for me, it was also a crisis of faith.

In the midst of my shock, disbelief, and grief, I began to search for answers. I studied the Scriptures. I read. I prayed. I talked to trusted Christian leaders. The whole question of how faith, prayer, healing, and God's will relate to each other became the central question of my life. And here is what I discovered.

To begin with, we must first recognize that faith in Christ is essential (for all aspects of the Christian life). The writer of Hebrews tells us that without faith it is impossible to please God (Hebrews 11:6). Jesus chose to limit his healing ministry as he ministered in his hometown of Nazareth due to persistent unbelief (Matthew 13:58), and so therefore the Bible elevates the role of faith as an important element in healing.

Second, the Bible clearly also elevates the importance of prayer. In fact, it describes times when healing did not come to fruition due to the lack of steadfast, dependent prayer. The disciples learned this lesson from Jesus himself (Matthew 17:14–21). In a more generic sense, James makes it clear that there are times when we do not receive things from God simply because we have not asked (James 4:2).

Therefore, as James aptly states in our text, God looks for "prayer offered in faith" (5:15 NIV 1984). And we shouldn't restrict this only to our pursuit of spiritual renewal or physical healing; this should be the pattern for all of the Christian life. The believer is called to walk by faith (2 Corinthians 5:7) while at the same time remaining in a continual attitude of steadfast, dependent prayer (1 Thessalonians 5:17).

So how does all this apply to James 5:13–16? Doesn't the text seem to imply that if we call the elders of the church to pray over us and anoint us with oil, we have a guarantee that the sick person will be made well? A closer look is surely warranted.

First, let's start with the role of the elders. As the spiritual shepherds of the church, they are charged with tending to the needs of the flock. So it is right for them to come to the aid of someone who is in need. In no way does this exclude other believers from coming alongside to assist in spiritual and physical matters, but here James specifically says to call the elders, the pastors—the shepherds.

Why? Because you want someone who will pray over you who is spiritually wise, mature, knowledgeable in the Scriptures, and familiar with God's ways. These are all key factors in knowing how to pray rightly in these kinds of circumstances. Furthermore, these shepherds should be well versed in prayer and able to handle delicate information and difficult situations, all of which are dynamics that are quite common in moments like this.

Second, we notice that it is not only the duty of the elders to pray, but James also ascribes to them the role of anointing (or rubbing) the sick person with oil in the name of the Lord. Interestingly, olive oil was used in biblical times for medicinal purposes as a way to protect and condition the skin (cf., the story of the Good Samaritan in Luke 10).

But James is not telling the elders to come pray and give medical attention. There was another purpose for using oil in the Bible. Oil was also used as a symbolic way of setting a person apart or consecrating someone to God. Kings were anointed and priests were ordained with anointing oil to communicate that this person was committed and set apart for God, for God's purposes.

Therefore, when the elders prayed over and anointed a sick person they were saying in one sense that this person was being set apart for special attention from God while they prayed.

Accompanied by a time of confession, the anointing with oil symbolically communicates that this is a moment where the one who is weak or sick is being consecrated unto the Lord and is renewing their commitment to place all of their trust in him. In essence, they would be saying, "God, I belong to you. My life is yours. My body and soul are yours, and we are praying for you to strengthen and heal."

Notice all this is to be done *in faith* and *in the name of the Lord.* That phrase, *in the name of the Lord,* carries serious implications. First of all, it recognizes that Jesus Christ is the Sovereign Lord of all things and that his purposes and will far outweigh ours. Second, it recognizes that we come to him in prayer not on the basis of any merits of our own, but based on who he is and what he has done for us. Finally, Jesus taught in John 14:13 that asking for things in his name will always be directly linked to that which will bring glory to God.

So if we merge all this together, to pray in the name of the Lord is to recognize that he is sovereign in the matter, and that he will answer our prayers in ways that bring him the most glory. He may choose to heal someone in this life or he may not, and in some instances this may have nothing to do with the amount of faith and prayer that is being exercised on the part of the believer.

Even someone with a mature, spiritually rich faith who prays steadfastly does not have the power to usurp the sovereign will of God if it is his will not to heal or to call a Christian home to heaven (and as Paul aptly says in Philippians 1:23, the latter is far better).

For example, Paul pleaded with God in 2 Corinthians 12 to take away a "thorn" in his flesh that had become a bother to his ministry. (Though we can't be too sure what this "thorn" was, I suspect it may have been an eye problem.) Nevertheless, this great apostle pleaded with God to relieve him of this difficulty, but the Lord basically said, "No, Paul, my grace is sufficient for you. My power is made perfect and is on display in the midst of your weakness."

Now we know that having much faith is better than having little faith, but let's be careful of telling someone that their loved one is still sick or may have died because they did not have enough faith to make the healing happen. We don't have God's perspective on that, and besides, how is that helpful during someone's time of grief? It seems pretty insensitive to me.

There are times when it is not God's will to physically heal in certain situations, and on those occasions we have to trust him and his goodness while relying on the sufficiency of his grace to carry us. The deciding factor is whether or not our request is in keeping with God's will (cf. 1 John 5:14–15).

But here the question naturally comes up. If God is sovereign and his will is going to be done anyway, why pray at all? Simple. Because God said we should. And sometimes the means that God uses to unlock his grace and healing power is in the context of our prayers. The consistent testimony of the Bible is that prayer makes a difference. James 5:16 says, "The prayer of a righteous man is powerful and effective" (NIV 1984).

So God, in his sovereignty, somehow takes into consideration and weaves into his plan the idea that we are praying in faith for his will to be done. Prayer matters, and when he does choose to heal (as I believe he still does today), often it is in response to faith-filled, persistent prayer.

Now someone may still ask, "I understand all that stuff about God's sovereignty and will and sufficient grace, but doesn't James still guarantee healing?" Well, yes, but *what kind of healing* is guaranteed? Look closer at the text.

To be fair, I don't think we can ever dismiss the possibility of physical healing being in view here, especially since James uses the imagery of the medicinal practice of anointing with oil along with the picture of someone being "raised up" (presumably from a position of lying down, as in a bed). But even if physical healing is in view here, we know that it is still conditional to all that we've said until now. (And though we prayed over and anointed my father, the Lord chose to take him home.)

Therefore, the more likely interpretation of what James is promising here is nothing less than a *spiritual restoration and healing.* There are two different Greek words that James uses in the text that are translated into the word *sick.* Looking elsewhere in the New Testament, these words can also communicate the idea of someone who is emotionally weary or spiritually weak due to persecution or suffering.

This would fit the context of the book of James well. The immediate surrounding context also suggests that James has more spiritual issues in mind here rather than physical ones. This is due to the fact that he talks about the confession of sin and the subsequent forgiveness that is sure to follow.

As soon as James mentions the prayer of faith that will make the sick person well, he says, "If he has sinned, he will be forgiven" (5:15 NIV 1984). Surely then, we are talking about a promise of spiritual restoration and spiritual healing that comes as a result of confession and faith-filled prayer. And that's why James continues:

> Therefore confess your sins to each other and pray for each other so that you may be healed. (James 5:16 NIV 1984)

So the only kind of healing that is absolutely guaranteed in this life is the spiritual healing and restoration that comes as a result of repentance and faith. God promises to spiritually restore and make us whole again. Sin has acted as a barrier, and may have even caused us to be physically weak (see 1 Corinthians 11:29–30). But spiritual healing comes to those who confess and turn from sin.

As Peter said in his sermon in the book of Acts, we should "repent, then, and turn to God, so that [our] sins may be wiped out, that times of refreshing may come from the Lord" (Acts 3:19 NIV 1984).

So even though physical healing is not guaranteed in this life, spiritual healing and restoration *is* guaranteed for those who repent of their sins and seek the Lord in faith. He is the Lord who will "raise them up," so that they may be spiritually made whole and restored again. Now, to be fair, God may in fact choose to physically heal someone who prays in faith for healing, but as we noted earlier, that will be answered according to God's sovereign will. And even if he chooses to do so, we know that our ultimate physical healing will have to wait for the life we inherit in the age to come.

I miss my dad. No question about it. As you can imagine, the day I prayed over and anointed him is a day I will never forget. And even though I was standing over him, in many ways I feel as if he was standing over me, affirming me with his love. I take comfort in the fact that in the days before his death, he enjoyed a true sense of spiritual renewal and restoration that came from confessing his sins and putting James 5 into practice. He truly was healed, in the way that matters most.

CHAPTER 15

Repent and Be Baptized

"Repent and be baptized every one of you in the name of
Jesus Christ for the forgiveness of your sins, and you will
receive the gift of the Holy Spirit."

—ACTS 2:38

INSTANT STRESS. That's how I feel when I pull into a restau-
rant's drive-through lane with a car full of people. Four
different orders, time needed to look at the menu, and a
person on the other side of the speaker who is asking me
after every item, "Does that complete your order?" Couple
that with the line of cars behind me full of people who are
tired of waiting, and I am not doing quite as well as I was a
mere five minutes earlier.

Then there are the things that puzzle me. The voice of the
person who welcomed me when I first pulled up is not the
same voice of the person who takes my order. Also, I am not

sure why an iced coffee costs more than a hot cup of coffee with a separate cup of ice (which is usually free).

Then there's the sales pitch, the add-ons: "Would you like to have an extra side of large fries with that for another 99 cents?" I know they have to ask, and all I have to say is *No, thank you*, but I'd rather not be faced with the temptation to spend more money. It reminds me of the feelings that come over me whenever I go through the oil change/car wash place and they come out to see me with my soiled air filter in their hands. *Do I really need a new one, or is this merely a way for them to siphon me?*

Today the "add-on" marketing strategy has reached new heights of creativity in order to get us to buy more of what we don't need. I recently heard a radio ad that declared, "Remember, the more you spend the more you save," which seems more than a little deceptive. But this is how many companies make their money, and many people are naïve enough to take the bait.

When it comes to matters of faith and doctrine, though, we should be very wary of add-ons. Such is the case with another commonly misused and misinterpreted passage of Scripture that originates out of the book of Acts. The misunderstanding of this verse has led to a line of false teaching that is ultimately very dangerous because it makes our salvation contingent upon human works (in this case, baptism). But this is not what the passage is teaching.

The text in question is found in Acts 2:38, where Peter is preaching his very first evangelistic sermon following the giving of the Holy Spirit at Pentecost. Filled with the Spirit, Peter's powerful sermon brings deep conviction to the people of Israel who have been "cut to the heart" over their realization that they are responsible for the murder of their chosen Messiah.

In the midst of their guilt and shame, the remorseful Jews plead with Peter and the disciples to tell them what they should do. Peter responds with authority:

> Repent and be baptized every one of you in the name of Jesus Christ for the forgiveness of your sins, and you will receive the gift of the Holy Spirit. (Acts 2:38)

The proper interpretation and application of this passage is that Peter is calling them to display their change of heart by completely renouncing and forsaking their sin (repentance) while at the same time turning *to* Christ in faith (the latter of which is implied). Biblically speaking, this is tantamount to expressing saving faith in Jesus Christ for the forgiveness of sin. It is one complete and simultaneous act (two sides of the same coin), which the apostle Paul confirmed later when he said that his ministry of the gospel was all about

> testifying both to Jews and to Greeks of *repentance* toward God and of *faith* in our Lord Jesus Christ. (Acts 20:21)

Both repentance and faith are gifts of God (Acts 5:31; 2 Timothy 2:25; Ephesians 2:8–9), which the believing sinner exercises in response to the gospel message. This is what Bible-believing Christians call the moment of conversion, whereby God grants new spiritual life to a dead heart (Ephesians 2:1), or as Jesus said, that moment when one is "born again" (John 3:3).

This is an amazing sovereign work of God (John 1:13), and it's in this moment that we become a "new creation"

(2 Corinthians 5:17), for the Holy Spirit brings us new life (John 3:6; 6:63), washes and renews us (Titus 3:5), and comes to permanently dwell in us (2 Corinthians 1:22; Ephesians 1:13–14). Therefore, as Peter says, not only do we receive forgiveness for sin, we receive the gift of the Holy Spirit himself—two amazing promises.

As a way to publicly declare their repentance (and faith) in a definitive sense, Peter also included the command to be baptized (an outward symbol of the inward cleansing done by God). This would have been a powerful visible symbol of the sincerity of their repentance, and it would vividly picture the spiritual cleansing that is taking place as the Spirit washes them of their sin (Titus 3:5). It is a subsequent act that has no saving power in and of itself, for we are saved by faith alone, so that no man may boast (Ephesians 2:8–9).

Yet here is where a large-scale misunderstanding has taken place that has resulted in this Scripture being misused to support a false line of teaching. Many who read this erroneously conclude that baptism is a necessary condition for salvation. For Peter did say, "Repent and be baptized . . . for the forgiveness of your sins." But to include baptism as a necessary condition for salvation would be to pit this interpretation against the entire teaching of the New Testament, where the Scriptures clearly teach that we are saved by faith alone (John 1:12; Galatians 2:16; Ephesians 2:8–9; Philippians 3:9). This we cannot do, because the Bible does not contradict itself.

Furthermore, if baptism were necessary for salvation then the thief on the cross was not really saved (since he did not have time to be baptized before his death), and Jesus would be a liar since he promised him that on that day the thief would be with him in paradise (Luke 23:43).

Throughout the remainder of the book of Acts, forgiveness is connected with repentance and faith (Acts 5:31; 10:43; 13:38–39). Peter later commanded, "Repent therefore, and turn back, that your sins may be blotted out" (Acts 3:19), and this he said without any mention of baptism. Additionally, when the Philippian jailer asked Paul what he must do to be saved, Paul simply said, "Believe in the Lord Jesus, and you will be saved" (Acts 16:31), and this is where the command stopped. Baptism then followed only as a testimony to his genuine conversion and the cleansing that he had received, and following through with it was an act of obedience to the teachings of Christ (Matthew 28:19).

But perhaps most insightful is the account of the conversion of Cornelius, the first Gentile convert who came to faith under Peter's preaching. In Acts 10, Peter preaches the gospel to Cornelius, who believed and was saved (with the reception of the Holy Spirit as evidence). It was only after this event took place that Peter asked:

> "Can anyone withhold water for baptizing these people, who have received the Holy Spirit just as we have?" And he commanded them to be baptized in the name of Jesus Christ. Then they asked him to remain for some days. (Acts 10:47–48)

Therefore, baptism is not *the means* of salvation, but rather is closely tied as the *subsequent symbol* of it. Even Peter would later say in one of his letters that it is not the outward act of baptism itself that saves you, but saving faith in Jesus Christ, the kind of faith that cleanses the conscience. And the washing and inner cleansing of our hearts (which includes our conscience) is what baptism is meant to symbolize and represent (1 Peter 3:21).

Beware then of add-ons, the idea that we should add something else besides faith to the idea of salvation. It is not biblical. We are saved by grace through faith alone.[1] In the book of Galatians, the false teachers wanted to add circumcision as a necessary add-on to saving faith, and this infuriated Paul. He asked them, "Are you so foolish? Having begun by the Spirit, are you now being perfected by the flesh?" (Galatians 3:3).

In other words, why do you think that the Holy Spirit's work in your salvation is not good enough and therefore find it necessary to "add on" something else (like an Old Testament law) in order to win God's favor in salvation?

The principle that once again surfaces in this example of a misused verse (Acts 2:38) is that it is always important to let Scripture interpret Scripture. In this case it teaches us that a surface reading of a text may not mean what we think it means if it cannot be corroborated anywhere else in the Bible. This should raise a red flag of caution for us.

Remember, unlike the voice at the drive-through, the voice that speaks in the pages of Scripture is the same voice that speaks from beginning to end. It is the voice of the Holy Spirit, and he is always consistent. And when it comes to salvation, there are no add-ons. Thanks be to God! For one thing, it is less stressful that way.

CHAPTER 16

Guarding Your Heart

"Above all else, guard your heart, for it is the wellspring of life."

—PROVERBS 4:23 NIV 1984

I WONDER IF YOU HAVE a friend who tends to back away from relationships whenever someone gets too personal or close. Does anyone come to mind? I can think of many, and I'm going to assume you can too. In fact, it's possible that I am describing you. Let's face it. For a variety of reasons, some people find it difficult to open up and share their thoughts and innermost feelings about life, experiences, relationships, and so on.

In some cultures, emotional vulnerability can be perceived as a sign of weakness, and therefore a more stoic or intellectual approach to life is often preferred or valued. If you have ever traveled the world or have ever lived in a highly diverse ethnic society, you quickly learn that some people groups tend not to like to share their innermost feelings. To use a common expression, they like to hold their cards close to their chest.

Yet to be fair, this can be more than a mere cultural phenomenon. There are many who have been raised in families where talking about matters of the heart was simply not done. Still others have been wounded by an unhealthy relationship, and this has caused them to recoil and refrain from being emotionally intimate with others.

Whatever the case, some by nature feel embarrassed or threatened to open their lives and hearts to others, and may hide behind careers, events, and activities. Behind their busyness is a loneliness that runs deep within their veins, though they would be the last ones to admit it.

It is in this context that we sometimes hear an oft-misused proverb tossed around to legitimize being standoffish:

> Above all else, guard your heart, for it is the wellspring of life. (Proverbs 4:23)

The natural question is what does the writer of Proverbs mean when he says that we should guard our hearts? Was he talking about the potential dangers of romantic love? Was he discouraging emotional vulnerability of any kind?

For starters, the book of Proverbs is a book of wisdom, a collection of sayings that give instructions on how to live a life that shuns evil and honors God. These sayings often originate out of the experiences of the author, and as mentioned earlier, they should be viewed as general life principles rather than guaranteed promises. They represent truths that when followed are not only helpful in guiding one's actions but also serve as healthy instructions for character development.

They are the seeds of sound teaching that when watered and applied help to cause a person to grow and develop into a mature, godly person.

With this in mind, it is important to realize that in the first nine chapters of the book of Proverbs, the author takes on the role of a father speaking to a son, instructing him on the benefits of wisdom and knowledge that are lived out in reverential fear of the Lord. This wisdom finds its roots in a relationship with God. In this way, it is more than just "head knowledge" that is being passed down within these proverbs. Rather, the teaching serves as the basis for an obedient life that is committed to worshiping God.

It is within this context that we find the "father's" instruction to the "son" that he should avoid the path of wickedness and evil. It is not a road that should ever be traveled upon, for it is a dangerous road of darkness that will cause one to stumble and fall. However, the road to long life, security, and well-being is found when one embraces the teachings and sayings of the wise father whose counsel provides protection and blessing for the one who heeds his words.

Here then is where our passage finds its context. The young son is advised to pay close attention to the words of the father so that his steps will be well established and firm so as to avoid evil. Using the parts of the body to illustrate his points, the father then instructs the boy to protect and guard his heart, to put away crooked and perverse speech from his lips, to fix his eyes straight to avoid distraction, and to ponder the paths of his feet so that his steps are well established and firm.

In Jewish literature, the word for *heart* is an all-encompassing term that includes the mind, the emotions, and the will. It is the center of one's being and the source from which all actions come, or as the proverb aptly calls it, "the wellspring of life." In other words, actions first find their roots within the depths of the heart. For even Jesus said in Matthew 12:34 that it is "out of the overflow of the heart that the mouth speaks."

Therefore, to "guard the heart" is to protect one's life from unhealthy influences that can easily corrupt our character. Applied to our world today, this might include things like pornography, gambling, or the abuse of alcohol. It may even cause us to take special notice of the friendship circles that we find ourselves in. For as the apostle Paul says in 1 Corinthians 15:33, "Bad company corrupts good character" (NIV 1984).

In the book of Proverbs, the author takes great strides to warn his son of the dangers of sexual promiscuity and adultery, which could destroy his character and ruin his life. For it is only in the safe pastures of marital fidelity that a man will find joy and satisfaction. Sexual passion is good, as long as it's kept in its proper context. For once the fire gets out of the fireplace (its proper place), it does nothing but burn everything it touches.

This passage, then, has nothing to do with hiding one's feelings. It can never be used as a verse to argue that one should be overly cautious in emotionally engaging others. Rather it is a passage that is all about preserving and protecting one's character from the evil that can quickly lead someone out of step with the kind of righteous living that honors God and brings blessing. This could mean the difference between life and death, success and failure.

In the ministry, you meet all kinds of people. Some are quiet, some are loud. Some are overly sensitive, some are a bit hardened. Some wear their hearts on their sleeves, and some are hard nuts to crack. But either way, we're all designed to live in relationships. This is how God designed us: to live in community, to live in harmony, to live in relationship with each other such that we can mutually love and care for one another as members of the body of Christ.

Inevitably, relationships involve risk, and yes, there will be times when we may get hurt or become disappointed with certain relationships, but we must be careful not to go inward to the point where we cannot experience deep personal, spiritual, and relational connection with someone else.

And guarding your heart is not a valid excuse to distance yourself from people or to refuse to allow someone else into your life. As we have seen, that's not even what it means.

Now, to be fair, certain types of people tend to be more on the intellectual rather than emotional side of things. And there is nothing wrong with that. There is a whole host of personality types that have all been uniquely made by God. Even so, we should never be as concerned with relationships as much as we should guard against the things in this corrupt world that stain us. It is in this context that we must always with God's help seek to guard our hearts.

CHAPTER 17

Where There Is No Vision

"Where there is no vision, the people perish."
—PROVERBS 29:18 KJV

WHY SO MANY DIFFERENT **B**IBLES? This question often surfaces in people's minds when they go to a bookstore to pick out a new Bible. There are thinline Bibles, reference Bibles, study Bibles, topical Bibles, and on and on. It is here where we enter into the world of translation philosophies, the theological angles taken in the study notes, format, print size, color, leather, hardback, thickness, etc. You name it, it's likely available.

A new believer is bound to be overwhelmed in choosing a Bible without help from someone familiar with all the different translations and paraphrases. But even for longtime Christians, the number of Bible options can be harrowing.

145

(Personally, I prefer the more literal word-for-word translation of the English Standard Version.)

When I consider the early church and the limited number of copies of the Scriptures available to them, I can't help but marvel about how blessed we truly are to have all this access to the inspired Word of God. We have instant access to it on the Internet as well as full copies of it on our smart phones. But aside from this, there is still another excellent question that surfaces from time to time that deserves an answer: Why is it necessary to always be updating or coming out with new translations of the Bible?

There are certainly many different reasons, but the best answer is this: *because language changes*. If there is one thing that is always moving, always changing, it is human language.

Let me give you an example. What if ten years ago I came up to you and asked, "So, are you and your family changing the type of light bulbs in your house so that you can *go green*?" A decade ago that would not have made sense. "What are you talking about?"

Is going green the same as wearing a Notre Dame T-shirt to a football game or painting your face green for St. Patrick's Day? No, today the idea of going green has everything to do with using products that are environmentally friendly such that they limit energy use, minimize waste, and encourage recycling, all the while seeking to save our natural resources (as much as is possible).

Therefore, the idea of going green is a relatively new idea, and the word *green* itself has a different set of connotations depending on its context. This is why dictionaries are being updated constantly. And in the same way that words can take on new meanings, words can lose or become detached from their former meanings.

An example of this is the word *conversation*. In today's usage, conversation is mainly understood as two or more people talking with one another in some sort of discussion or verbal exchange of ideas. But many years ago, the word *conversation* had a different connotation. It was mainly used to describe a person's way of life or behavior.

For example, in observing their growing child, a wife may have said to her husband, "It certainly is noteworthy to see how our son's conversation has changed over the years, don't you think?" And of course they would be referring to his overall behavior and manner of living, and not necessarily to the things they often hear him say. But that's not how we would use the word *conversation* today. That usage seems somewhat archaic to us.

With all this in mind then, it's understandable why it might be necessary to have updated versions of the Bible due to the fact that some English words may have changed or lost their contextual meanings. It is with these thoughts in mind that we turn to another widely misused Bible verse, Proverbs 29:18.

Here is a case where an archaic usage and understanding of an English word within the King James Version of the Bible has led to so many people misunderstanding and misusing what is truly a powerful verse of Scripture. Though the King James is still a reliable translation, modern-day readers often have difficulty in conceptualizing what is being communicated unless they are familiar with its antiquated language. I will first present Proverbs 29:18 from the King James Version and then explain what is really being said. Here's how the first half of the verse reads:

Where there is no vision, the people perish. (KJV)

I'm guessing you have heard this verse cited before, and the reason so many quote the King James Version is that it is convenient to use its wording to support many modern-day ideas and agendas. Based on a surface reading of it, the verse seems to be talking about *having a vision for a planned out future.* The idea being if we don't have a plan for success in the immediate future, then we're bound to fail, or in this extreme case, "perish." But this is not what this verse means. But before we explain what it does mean, let's talk about *vision.*

This notion of having a vision is widely used today in many circles. For example, as Americans we often elect our national politicians to serve in public office based on their vision for the country's future.

In a slightly different way, companies often have to sit down as leaders and envision what or where they want their company to be five, ten, or twenty years from now. Then they develop a vision statement along with an accompanying strategy and tactics in order to obtain this anticipated future. Even churches today talk about having a vision for their particular church so that all their programs and activities are aimed at a set of clearly defined, desired goals.

So when someone finds a passage of Scripture that at first glance may support the idea of needing a vision, there is an immediate temptation to grab hold of it and use it. After all, wouldn't it be great to find biblical warrant for this kind of visionary strategic planning? Yes, perhaps it would. But the fact of the matter is there's still a major problem with using *this* verse *that* way.

Plain and simple, this verse is not talking about future strategic planning. Even though it's tempting to hijack this verse to support that idea, it would be a misuse of the author's intent. All you have to do is look in almost any other translation of the Bible in order to see what the verse is really saying. In fact let's just quickly compare Proverbs 29:18 translations:

> Where there is no vision, the people perish. (King James Version)

> Where there is no revelation, the people cast off restraint. (New King James Version and New International Version 1984)

> Where there is no prophetic vision, the people cast off restraint. (English Standard Version)

Now you can clearly see that some of the more recent translations give out a much different idea of what the verse is saying than what we read in the older King James Version. It almost sounds as if the other versions are quoting a different verse, but they are not. I would argue the other translations provide a much better sense of what is being truly communicated within the original Hebrew text.

Let's use the New International Version (1984), which says, "Where there is no revelation, the people cast off restraint." Perhaps it would be even more helpful to cite the entire verse in its full context:

> Where there is no revelation, the people cast off restraint; but blessed is he who keeps the law.

This verse is discussing *the divine revelation of God* that has come down to us from heaven. It's about how God has chosen to speak to humankind by means of supernatural revelation, the revelation that was directly given by God to the prophets and apostles of old who wrote it down for us, which is what our Bible is today.

But four hundred years ago, when the King James Version first came out, the English translators of the Bible in seventeenth-century England chose to use the word *vision* instead of the word *revelation* when referring to God's supernatural communication to his people. This would have been an appropriate translation of the original Hebrew text of Scripture, especially since God communicated to his prophets by means of visions, dreams, and oracles. And the readership of that day would have understood that *vision* meant *revelation*.

However, in our modern-day American culture, the word *vision* has many more meanings. It can refer to a person's eyesight. It can refer to a supernatural experience of divine revelation, and as I have said, it can also refer to having a long-term strategic goal and plan for a business or a company.

Here, then, is where things can go awry. The misuse of Proverbs 29:18 arises when we randomly take one of the modern-day uses of the word *vision* (like having a business plan) and illegitimately import that idea back into the biblical text in a way that is completely foreign to the author's original intent. And that's what has happened with the misinterpretation and misuse of this verse. It is being hijacked and misused all in an effort to support the modern-day idea of the need for a corporate vision for an organization (even a church's vision).

I find it interesting that the *New* King James Version, an update to the original King James Version, changes the translation altogether. It now uses the word *revelation* instead of the word *vision*. I can't help but wonder if the scholars who oversaw and implemented the update sought to avoid the common confusion that often surrounds this verse.

So what does it mean to say that without divine revelation, the people cast off restraint? Let me try to give some concrete thought on this and a relevant example.

When we as Christians are regularly engaged in reading and studying the Bible, the Holy Spirit uses that discipline to build us up and strengthen us in the faith. As our minds become fortified by the truths of God's Word, we learn how to think more like God. Furthermore, the Holy Spirit uses the power of God's Word to help us in our victory over sin. Psalm 119:11 says, "I have hidden your word in my heart that I might not sin against you" (NIV 1984).

What this means is that when God's Word is fixed in our hearts, it enables us to sort out right from wrong and enables us to practice restraint whenever we are tempted to sin. One can easily say that when God's Word is heeded and obeyed, it has protective value. It protects us from evil thoughts and behaviors and helps shape our moral boundaries so that we know how to live a life that pleases God.

On the other hand, when God's Word is ignored or missing altogether from someone's life, this ability to sort out right from wrong and to practice restraint is limited or missing. We are bound to fail and fall into patterns of sin. And this is what the writer of this proverb meant when he said, "Where there is no vision [prophetic revelation], the people cast off restraint." BUT, "blessed is he who keeps the law [God's Word]."

Let me give you an example of how this proverb can be applied and essentially rings true in our culture today. In the book of Genesis, we are taught that human beings were made in the image of God, both male and female alike. This implies that all of us have inherent value and that life is sacred. Therefore, we must do everything we can to care for and protect it. But the question naturally surfaces, when does this life begin? The moment we are born, or much earlier? Thankfully, the Bible has a clear answer.

In Psalm 51, King David was confessing his sin, and in the midst of his confession he made some profound statements. He first admitted he was a sinner. But more than that, he said that he was sinful from the time *his mother conceived him*. This is profoundly significant, for it teaches us that life and personhood must certainly begin the moment we are conceived. At least that's how David, speaking under the inspiration of the Holy Spirit, understood his life.

This in turn helps us sort out what is right and wrong and why we need to practice restraint when it comes to the issue of abortion. Since life begins at conception, abortion is wrong because it ends a life that is inherently sacred (no matter what "stage" that life is in). It is a life that has been created in the image of God that is only different from you and me in terms of its location (in the womb) and in its stage of development. Other than that, it is a living soul.

On the other hand, for those who do not know (or care to know) the teaching of the Bible concerning this, there is little reason to have such convictions or to practice restraint on abortion. This makes the proverb essentially prophetic, for it is indeed describing the current state of affairs in a secular culture that has little regard for the Word of God and shows an increasing disinterest in practicing moral restraint. It amazes me how much Scripture still speaks to and describes sinful human nature today, even hundreds or thousands of years after it was written.

In conclusion, the Bible rightly understood and applied has a way of protecting us, setting our moral compass, and restraining us from patterns of sin. It teaches us right from wrong and helps us to become discerning in our quest to please God in all things. Blessed indeed is the one who believes, keeps, and follows God's law. Those who do so experience life!

And as far as good business planning goes and developing a corporate vision, it is a noble thing to do, but it can't be mandated or appealed to on the basis of Proverbs 29:18. We must be careful of reading our own agendas back into a text that was not designed for the purposes that we are so eager to use it for.

CHAPTER 18

Lifting Up the Name of Jesus

"And I, when I am lifted up from the earth, will draw all people to myself."

—JOHN 12:32

SOMETIMES IT IS SO TEMPTING to quote verses that seem to "fit." Let me explain.

I am a big fan of handwritten letters. In the age of computers, copiers, faxes, emails, and Facebook messages, the privilege of seeing a loved one's unique handwriting is waning fast. But there seems to be something very personal and meaningful in it. When was the last time you received a letter in the mail that was fully written by hand? Can't remember? Not surprising.

I remember when I was in college, I sent my parents a letter in the mail to tell them how things were going and I made the mistake of only *typing* my first name at the end of the letter. Boy, did my mother ever correct me. I can still hear her voice today in my head, saying, "Hey, I want to see you sign your name." Perhaps she was right in insisting on this lest my correspondence become impersonal and detached. My fear today is that email and instant messages have done just that.

So hypothetically speaking, if I wanted to make a strong case that we should avoid email because it is still important to write handwritten letters to loved ones, wouldn't it be great if I could find a Bible verse that would support my cause? Interestingly, this is what people often do when they misuse Scripture. They come up with a plan or an argument and then try to go back and find a Bible verse that seems to fit or support what they are trying to assert.

Now, if this approach were valid (and I am arguing that *it is not*), then here's what I'd pull out to support my case. Paul's closing words to some of his letters seem to suit my agenda well. Take a look at some of these cleverly extracted verses:

See with what large letters I am writing to you with my own hand. (Galatians 6:11)

Now may the Lord of peace himself give you peace at all times in every way. The Lord be with you all. I, Paul, write this greeting with my own hand. This is the sign of genuineness in every letter of mine; it is the way I write. (2 Thessalonians 3:16–17)

All the brothers send you greetings. . . . I, Paul, write this greeting with my own hand. (1 Corinthians 16:20–21)

In these verses, it is important to note what Paul is doing. He often dictated his letters, but in order to prove the authenticity of the letter or in order to say a personal farewell (see also Colossians 4:18), Paul would, on occasion, pick up the pen himself and sign it with his own hand. He was not making a biblical case for handwritten letters. Why, you ask? Because all they had back then were handwritten letters.

So you can see that it would be quite unnatural and a major stretch for me to pull this out of context and use it to support a personal agenda that seeks to abolish emails and take us back to the days of handwritten letters (though I have no such agenda). Yet this is the way Scripture is often misused and abused today.

This leads me to a case of another misused Scripture that is often cited in the context of leading worship in the church. It is John 12:32:

> And I, when I am lifted up from the earth, will draw all people to myself.

The words come from the lips of Jesus Christ, and on the surface, they would seem to fit the agenda of an overzealous worship leader who is seeking to "lift up the name of Jesus" in song as God's people gather and engage in worship.

Now, to be fair, *lift up* was a common biblical phrase used in the context of biblical worship, both in the Old and New Testaments. For example, in Isaiah 24 we are told that when the Lord judges the earth, the redeemed will "lift up their voices, they [will] sing for joy" (Isaiah 24:14). David, in Psalm 25, begins by saying, "To you, O Lord, I lift up my soul" (v. 1). And when the Hebrews ascended to Jerusalem for worship, they would sing, "I lift up my eyes to the hills. From where does my help come? My help comes from the Lord, who made heaven and earth" (Psalm 121:1–2).

In the New Testament, when Paul was giving instructions to Timothy about corporate worship, he stated, "In every place the men should pray, lifting holy hands without anger or quarreling" (1 Timothy 2:8). In other words, instead of hands that fight and are prone to anger, Paul wanted the men to live a holy life and lift up their hands to the Lord in prayer.

Furthermore, the Psalms tell us to "ascribe glory" to his name (Psalm 29:2), and to "magnify the Lord . . . exalt his name together!" (Psalm 34:3). We are "to sing the glory of his name" (Psalm 66:2). The list could go on, but you have the general idea: Figuratively speaking, believers are to "lift up" the name of the Lord as our hearts and minds worship him in song, and this is a perfectly legitimate thing to say when the church gathers for worship!

But we should be cautious using John 12:32, and here's why. In this context Jesus is nearing the end of his earthly ministry, the final week before his death. Though he knows his destiny, Jesus, as a man, is still troubled in his soul about what lies ahead. Yet he is also fully aware of the victory over evil that lies ahead when he goes to the cross to make atonement for human sin. He speaks of the judgment of evil, the defeat of Satan, and the triumph that will secure salvation for whosoever will believe (cf. John 3:14–15).

This latter idea is what is captured in John 12:32. Reading it again, Jesus says:

> And I, when I am lifted up from the earth, will draw all people to myself.

John tells us in the very next verse that "being lifted up" was Jesus' reference to his manner of death, i.e., crucifixion. For John comments in footnote fashion and says, "He said this to show by what kind of death he was going to die" (v. 33). Therefore, being lifted up was the equivalent of being hung on a cross. Jesus spoke of this idea earlier in the gospel of John when he said:

> And as Moses lifted up the serpent in the wilderness, so must the Son of Man be lifted up, that whoever believes in him may have eternal life. (John 3:14–15)[1]

So the idea of being "lifted up" has everything to do with Christ's crucifixion, a crucifixion that surely has in view his resurrection and ascension into glory that has come by way of the cross. And it is through this great work (atoning sacrifice) on the cross that Jesus will draw "all men" to himself, meaning that he will draw to himself men from every tribe, tongue, and nation (both Jew and Gentile), which is a common theme in this gospel account (cf. 6:44).

Therefore, if John 12:32 is referring to Jesus being "lifted up" in terms of his crucifixion, then we should be cautious about using it as a proof text for lifting him up and praising him in worship. We don't intend to "crucify" him all over again in our worship. If our intent is to lift him up (or lift up his name) in praise, there are several other verses that we can appeal to if we want to communicate that. So in short, I believe we can confidently say, "Right idea, wrong verse."

To be fair, it is easy to misuse Scripture this way even when the intentions are noble. And even though this verse sounds like it might support the worship leader's idea or agenda, it is not the best one suited for the task. Indeed, sometimes it is so tempting to quote verses that seem to "fit."

CHAPTER 19

Conclusion

Handle With Care—
Using Scripture Appropriately

WHEN THE APOSTLE PAUL charged his young disciple and protégé Timothy to carry on the work of the ministry, he made it clear the ministry of the gospel was to be founded upon the Word of God. Nothing else would do, for a ministry without the Word is not Christianity; it has morphed into something else.

Paul reassured Timothy that there is inherent power in the Word of God itself, God's revelation to us:

All Scripture is breathed out by God and profitable for teaching, for reproof, for correction, and for training in righteousness, that the man of God may be complete, equipped for every good work. (2 Timothy 3:16–17)

Timothy's ability to remain competent and fully equipped for his life and calling had everything to do with his constant faithfulness to and reliance upon the Word of God. "Breathed out by God," the fully inspired and inerrant Word is useful for teaching, rebuking, correcting, and training others in righteous living and godliness. And Paul was insistent that Timothy handle the Word with care, for it is a powerful weapon (as attested to elsewhere in Hebrews 4:12).

Paul wanted Timothy to be full of zeal, eager to show himself worthy of the task that was laid upon him, for Timothy was ultimately accountable to God. As he proclaimed and taught the Word, he was to "rightly handle the word of truth" (2 Timothy 2:15). In other words, he was to study, teach, and proclaim it with accuracy so as to "get it right."

Architects know that if building plans are off ever so slightly, it skews the entire design. Such is also true in handling the Word of God. It is vital that we seek to read, understand, interpret, and apply it correctly. Lives are at stake if we don't.

Common Mistakes That Lead to Misuse

Throughout this book, we have explored many important principles to keep and mistakes to avoid in order to interpret and apply the Bible properly. With respect to mistakes, oftentimes a mere partial or surface reading may be insufficient, and isolating a certain passage without reading the fuller context can result in a major misreading of the text. This easily explains how the "eye for eye" passage was misused even in Jesus' day.

Furthermore, it is important to use Scripture to interpret Scripture. As I have said before, God's Word never contradicts itself because God never contradicts himself. God is not the author of confusion, so if an interpretation doesn't match what is theologically taught elsewhere, we know it has not been interpreted correctly.

We must also resist the temptation to make a passage "work" how we want it to work or "make it say" what we want it to say. Many have fallen prey to this temptation and as such have read into Scripture what they want to see. You may recall this is what Hitler did when he hijacked the words of Jesus in order to condemn all Jews. He ripped Jesus' words of condemnation toward the hypocrisy and poison of the Pharisees out of its context, and he misapplied them to the entire Jewish people in a sweeping fashion—simply because that's what Hitler wanted them to say. This approach does not seek to draw out the meaning of a text but rather to "put in" the meaning that someone desires it to have.

We have also seen the dangers that come from misquoting a text (e.g., "Money is the root of all evil"). What someone adds in, or in this case, *leaves out*, when quoting a passage of Scripture is profoundly significant. This type of Scripture twisting, if you remember, is how the serpent in the book of Genesis deceived Adam and Eve.

Finally, be careful of inadequate understandings and implications of the gospel that are read back into certain passages. The gospel never promised we would always be in good health, financially wealthy, and prosperous in this life.[1] It doesn't promise blessing as is often defined by us in human terms or according to what we think is "good" for us now. So "plans to prosper you" (in a material sense) or to "make the sick person well" (in a physical sense) may be plans that aren't fully realized until the life to come.

The Faithful Task

In the task of interpreting and applying Scripture, our desire is to discover the mind of God on a matter. There can only be one proper interpretation of a text even though there may be numerous applications. During my college years, I attended several "Bible studies" in the dorm rooms of fellow students, and I vividly remember watching well-intentioned believers sit around and discuss what this or that passage "means to me."

Unfortunately, this merely became a pool of ignorance, where personal subjectivity at the expense of sound interpretive principles ruled the day. The proper question should not be "What does this passage mean to me?" but rather "What were the author's original intentions and how did the audience who first received it understand those intentions in the original context?" And then, only after discovering this is it appropriate to ask, "How then does the timeless biblical principle contained in this passage apply to me today?"

When we interpret any biblical text, we all come to the task with personal baggage and biases. We all have assumptions that come out of our life experiences and training, and these assumptions act as a filter for how we read a text. To be fair, this is to be expected of all of us, and being aware of what those biases are and how they may affect our perspective is crucial for proper interpretation and application.

However, it should be clear by now that discovering the context of any Scripture is the starting point for proper interpretation. This context ranges from the literary to the historical-cultural to the grammatical contexts. Understanding the meaning of words, grammatical relationships, and literary genres is essential in order to grasp the meaning of any text.

For example, when it comes to literary genres, the proverbs stand out as a unique style of literature that we must become familiar with in order to properly interpret and apply their truths. As discussed earlier, the nature of proverbs is that they are often general principles instead of hard and fast (or absolute) promises. Furthermore, there is a big difference between prophecy, poetry, narrative, parables, letters, apocalyptic literature, etc., and we would do well to become familiar with the unique characteristics of each.

As you learn to read the Bible in context, remember to always start with a literal reading of the text. Unless it is obvious that figurative language is being used, seek to understand the plain sense of every passage, looking up the meaning of words that you may not know or unfamiliar figures of speech.

Discovering the immediate context of the text comes by looking at the surrounding verses and the flow of thought found within those verses. A wider look at the chapter itself and the book as a whole provides additional perspective for interpretation. Asking the basic questions of who, what, when, where, and why will provide an investigative approach that helps you ascertain the author's original intent.

It is also important to understand the historical setting and cultural distinctions that surround the text itself. For example, discovering the worldview of the people, their family structures, political climates, economic conditions, geographical features, and customs are but a few of the areas that will aid in the task.

A wide array of study Bibles are available now that give much of this information in addition to information about the author, time, place, purpose, and major themes of each book. I highly recommend the *English Standard Version Study*

Bible as a major resource for the layperson. It is a virtual flood of information—cross references, maps, study notes, a concordance, and the list goes on (not to mention an excellent, reliable, essentially literal translation).

Today we have more resources than ever before as Bible dictionaries, commentaries, systematic theologies, surveys, and lexicons are readily available. A number of online resources can be accessed as well—but proceed here with caution. As you well know, we can't believe everything we read on the Internet.

All this said, it is important to understand that reading and studying the Bible involves not only proper interpretation but also proper application.

The Bible aims to teach us about God and ourselves and about his wonderful plan of salvation for humankind. God uses his Word to transform and change us. It is living and active. It shapes our minds, changes our hearts, and causes us to grow. Understanding and applying its timeless principles is part of what it means to be a man or woman of faith and a follower of Jesus Christ. But no believer can do this successfully unless he or she relies on the Holy Spirit to aid in interpretation and application. For it is the Spirit's unique role to lead us and "guide [us] into all the truth" (John 16:13).

Our humble dependency upon the Holy Spirit for understanding, illumination, and transformation as we read the Word is an essential component to faithful living for those who claim to be disciples. For the Spirit who lives in us is the same Spirit who inspired every word of Scripture. And as we forsake sin, surrender our hearts, and are filled with the Spirit, we will become increasingly saturated, equipped, and made wise with his truth (2 Timothy 3:15).

It was always Christ's desire that we be "people of the Word." For Jesus rightly said:

If you abide in my word, you are truly my disciples, and you will know the truth, and the truth will set you free. (John 8:31–32)

This, then, is God's will for us, that we rely upon the indwelling Holy Spirit and *seek the Lord in prayer* for assistance in interpreting and applying his Word. Furthermore, our ongoing fellowship with other faithful believers who are regularly reading, studying, and applying the Scriptures along with us is also essential. For Scripture is best understood, interpreted, and applied in the context of the Spirit-filled community of faith where sound interpretive methods are utilized.

Finally, I want to encourage you to understand the value of solid, biblical expository preaching. In churches where the Word of God is faithfully preached, our ability to interpret and apply Scripture faithfully in context receives an exponential boost. The ministry of the pulpit helps establish the culture of each church and through expository preaching, value is placed on God's Word as the central nourishing component to the Christian life.

God's Word is truth, and we are sanctified by his truth (John 17:17). It is a precious gift of God. May it be our prayer that we learn to use it faithfully and appropriately so that in all things God will be glorified. For if he returns today, may we be found faithful.

Notes

Chapter 1: Where It All Began

1. Adolf Hitler, in a speech in Munich, Germany, on April 12, 1922, as found on www.humanitas-international.org/showcase/chronography/speeches/1922-04-12.html. It is remarkable and deeply offensive to see that Hitler regarded himself as a Christian in this speech.

2. Though no person comes to the text completely unbiased and objective, we must nevertheless seek to use the proper methods of interpretation that the Bible itself outlines for us while checking our findings with the way it has been understood throughout church history. Proper care must be taken in handling what is regarded as a "two-edged sword" (Hebrews 4:12), lest we do great harm to the body of Christ. When correct interpretive methods are joined together with the internal testimony of the Spirit and the discerning spirit of the Christian community, we can rest assured that we have arrived at a text's proper meaning so that we can in turn apply it to our lives.

3. Some may surmise that Adam may have added that to the command as a way of adding additional protection to the restriction, but that is merely speculation.

Chapter 2: Judging Others

1. Mark Dever, "Biblical Church Discipline," *The Southern Baptist Journal of Theology*, Vol. 4, No. 4. Winter 2000, 39. Dever writes, "Could

it be that in our day, a misunderstanding of Matthew 7:1 has been a shield for sin and has worked to prevent the kind of congregational life that was known by the churches of an earlier day, and could be known by us again?"

Chapter 3: Plans to Prosper You and Not to Harm You

1. Paul warned Timothy about similar false teachers in 2 Timothy 4:3–4.

Chapter 5: Ask for Anything in My Name

1. It is true, however, that they as apostles ("sent ones") will be specially commissioned by Christ to perform supernatural signs and miracles as a testimony to their authority as God's unique messengers, which further authenticated the gospel message they proclaimed (cf. 2 Corinthians 12:12).

2. This will no doubt be due to the Holy Spirit's indwelling presence and influence, whose role is to illumine their minds, teach them, and remind them of the truths Jesus taught (John 14:26).

Chapter 6: Working All Things Together for Good

1. To be sure, all believers who die before the return of Christ will become fully sanctified (morally perfect like Christ) after their death as their soul enters into the presence of the Lord. However, we await the resurrection body at the return of Christ, and then we can confidently say that both body and soul have been glorified.

2. Though we will not deal directly with this, it is interesting to see that Paul defined all believers in Christ as those whom God *foreknew* and *predestined,* which tells us that God has been working for our good since before the creation of the world!

3. But lest we think that God's definition of good is all about *us,* we must remember that anything that glorifies God and advances his kingdom purposes could rightly be called *good,* but surely this also includes our transformation.

Chapter 8: Jesus As the Firstborn Over All Creation

1. Fritz Ridenour, *So What's the Difference? A Look at 20 Worldviews, Faiths and Religions and How They Compare to Christianity* (Ventura: Regal Books, 2001), *revised and expanded edition,* 123.

2. This was the teaching of Charles Taze Russell, founder of the Jehovah's Witnesses, who also denied the deity of the Holy Spirit and the

existence of hell, and who advocated that Christ spiritually (not literally) returned to earth in 1914, and is now spiritually reigning through the absolute authority of *Watchtower Society.*

Chapter 10: No More Than You Can Handle

1. John MacArthur Jr., *First Corinthians: The MacArthur New Testament Commentary* (Chicago: Moody Press, 1984), 228.

Chapter 11: Train Up a Child

1. Allen P. Ross, "Proverbs" in *The Expositor's Bible Commentary,* Vol. 5 (Grand Rapids: Zondervan, 1991), 1061.

2. Tremper Longman III, *Proverbs: Baker Commentary on the Old Testament Wisdom and Psalms* (Grand Rapids: Baker Academic, 2006), 405.

Chapter 13: An Eye for an Eye

1. It is worthy to note that in the ESV Study Bible, the commentary notes point out that God "distinguishes between death due to willful murder and death due to negligence" (see Exodus 21:12–14, 28–32), 178. Therefore, differing punishments were often meted out depending on circumstances.

Chapter 15: Repent and Be Baptized

1. Though it is true we are saved by grace through faith alone, this does not mean that works have no place, for good works are necessary to follow as evidence that saving faith exists. Martin Luther rightly said, "We are justified by faith alone, but not by a faith that is alone."

Chapter 18: Lifting Up the Name of Jesus

1. Jesus is referring to the account of Moses in Numbers 21:5–9, where Israel spoke rebelliously to Moses against the Lord and incurred divine judgment. The Lord's judgment was that poisonous snakes were sent to bite the Israelites, causing many to die. The people then confessed their sin and pleaded with Moses to intercede with the Lord on their behalf. Moses did so and the Lord commanded Moses to make a bronze serpent and lift it up on a pole before the people so that whosoever looked at it would be healed. The parallel that Jesus is making is that in the same way that people were *physically* healed by looking at that which was "lifted up," so it is true that *spiritual* healing and eternal life will come

to whosoever looks to the Son of Man in faith, the Son of Man who is crucified and "lifted up" on a cross.

Chapter 19: Conclusion: Handle With Care—Using Scripture Appropriately

1. The gospel *does*, however, promise many rich spiritual blessings (see 2 Peter 1:3–4, for example).

Eric J. Bargerhuff, PhD, teaches in the Bible and Theology department and directs the Honors Program at Trinity College of Florida. He served in pastoral ministry for more than twenty years in churches in Ohio, Illinois, and Florida. He received his doctorate in biblical and systematic theology from Trinity Evangelical Divinity School. Eric's passion is to write systematic and practical theology for the purposes of spiritual growth and reform in the church. He is a member of the Center for Pastor Theologians (CPT) and the Evangelical Theological Society (ETS).

Eric is the author of *The Most Misused Verses in the Bible* and *The Most Misused Stories in the Bible*. He also wrote *Love that Rescues: God's Fatherly Love in the Practice of Church Discipline*, which explores the grace and fatherly love of God that should be embodied in a church's efforts to restore a brother or sister in Christ who has gone astray.

Eric and his family live in Trinity, Florida.